D1488805

THE FACSIMILE TEXT SOCIETY

SERIES I: LITERATURE AND LANGUAGE

VOLUME 2

THOMAS WARTON THE ELDER

POEMS ON SEVERAL OCCASIONS

1748

THOMAS WARTON *The Elder*

POEMS

ON

SEVERAL OCCASIONS

Reproduced from the Edition of 1748

THE FACSIMILE TEXT SOCIETY

NEW YORK

1930

Printed in the United States of America
by The National Process Company, New York

BIBLIOGRAPHICAL NOTE

Poems On Several Occasions by Thomas Warton the Elder is reproduced from a copy in the New York. Public Library. This copy has been collated with the copy in the library of Harvard University; the two copies have been found to be identical.

F.A.P.

POEMS

ON

SEVERAL OCCASIONS.

By the REVEREND

Mr. *THOMAS WARTON*,

BATCHELOR of DIVINITY,

Late Vicar of *Basingstoke* in *Hampshire*,
and sometime Professor of Poetry in the
University of *Oxford*.

Nec lusisse pudet.   HOR.

LONDON:

Printed for R. MANBY and H. S. COX, on *Ludgate-
Hill.* M.DCC.XLVIII.

TO THE

RIGHT HONOURABLE

FULWAR CRAVEN,

Lord CRAVEN, *Baron of* HAMP-
STEAD MARSHALL.

My LORD,

I BEG Leave to put the following POEMS
under the Protection of your Lordſhip;
as the Perſon for whom the deceaſed Author
had the juſteſt Veneration and Reſpect;
and to whom He himſelf would have choſen
to inſcribe his Writings as a Memorial of
the Friendſhip with which your Lordſhip
condeſcended to honour Him. He often
reflected with Pleaſure on the unſhaken In-

tegrity

tegrity and unbiass'd Patriotism of your
Lordship; who with a matchless Singularity
has maintain'd the glorious Independence
of a Truly *British* Nobleman, in an Age
of universal Venality and Corruption. Nor
was He less charm'd with the strict Justice,
and Oeconomy, that Constancy in Friend-
ship, and that Affability and Benevolence
which adorn your Lordship's private Life.

That you may long continue an Ornament
and Support to your Country which wants
your Example, is the most sincere Wish of,

My LORD,

Your LORDSHIP'S

Most Obliged,

and Most

Obedient Servant,

J. WARTON.

SUBSCRIBERS.

A.

THE Right Honourable the Lady Anne Acton.
  Sir Richard Atkyns, *Bart.*
John Abdy, *Esq;*
Miss Abdy.
Miss Charlotte Abdy.
Mrs. Adams.
Miss Adams.
Miss Betty Adams.
Mr. Austen, *of* St. John's *College* Oxford.
Master Francis Annesley, *of* Bucklebury, Berks.
Master Arthur Annesley, *of* Bucklebury, Berks.
Mrs. Cat. Arden, *of* Cheshire.
Miss Arden.
Rev. Mr. John Acton, *Rector of* Walton upon the
  Hill, Surrey.
Mrs. Alcroft, *of* Mitcham *in* Surrey.
Rev. Mr. Alcock, *of* Trotton *in* Sussex.
—— Addington, *M. D. of* Reading, Berks.
Rev. Mr. Brian Allott, *of* Lanesbourgh, Yorkshire.

B.

The Rt. Hon. *the* Lady Bingley.

William Bowyear, *Esq;*

Rev. Mr. Bigg, *of* Worting, Hants. 6 *Books.*

Mrs. Baniſter.

Mr. Robert Burgeſs, *of* All Souls *College*, Oxford.

Mr. Walter Bartlet, *of* Univerſity *College*, Oxford.

Mr. George Baker, *of* Oriel *College*, Oxford.

Edward Blake, *A. M. Fellow of* Oriel *College*, Oxford.

Edward Bentham, *B. D. Fellow of* Oriel *College*, Oxford.

Mr. George Barnes, *Com*ʳ. *of* Oriel *College*, Oxford.

Charles Blackſtone, *LL. B. Fellow of* New *College*, Oxford.

Mr. Blackſtone, *Fellow of* All Souls *College*, Oxford.

Rev. William Burrows, *B. D. Fellow of* St. John's *College*, Cambridge.

Mrs. Bayly, *of* Newington, Oxfordſhire.

Nathaniel Booth, *Esq;*

Miſs Barnes, *of* Soho.

Rev. Mr. Brooke, *of* Tong *in* Yorkſhire.

Rev. Mr. John Butler, *Rector of* Wateringbury *in* Kent.

Mr. Samuel Barwick, *of* London.

Mrs. Bourchier, *of* Chicheſter.

Mrs. Barton, *of* St. Andrews. 3 *Books.*

John Bilderbeck, *Esq;*

Mr. Baker.

Mr. Bonnam.

Thomas

Thomas Beaumont, *Esq; of* Dalton *in* Yorkshire.

Samuel Burrows, *Esq; Master in Chancery.* 2 *Books.*

Mr. Bowle, *Com^r of* Oriel *College*, Oxford.

Mr. Rob. Bell, *Gentleman Commoner of* St. Mary's Hall, Oxford.

C.

The Rt. Hon. the Lord Carteret.

The Hon. Josiah Child, *Esq;*

—— Chapman, *A. M. Fellow of* Trinity *College*, Oxford.

—— Carne, *A. M. of* Trinity *College*, Oxford.

—— Camplyn, *A. M. of* Queen's *College*, Oxford.

Mr. John Clerke.

John Cooper, *A. M. Fellow of* Oriel *College*, Oxford.

Washington Cotes, *A. M. Fellow of* Oriel *College*, Oxford.

Arthur Culme, *A. M. Fellow of* Baliol *College*, Oxford.

Mr. Henry Corker, *Commoner of* Queen's *College*, Oxford.

—— Creffield, *A. M. Fellow of* Magdalen *College*, Oxford.

Mr. Clarke.

Charles Cole, *Esq;*

Mr. John Carter, *Clerk of the King's Victualling Office in* London.

John Cookson, *of* Wakefield, *M. D.*

Mrs. Copeley, *of* Wakefield, *Widow.*

Mrs. Henrietta Currer.

Mr. Crowder.

Mr.

Mr. Chamberlain, *of* Skipton, Yorkſhire.
Mr. Baylis Caſberd, *of* St. John's *College in* Oxford.
Miſs Chitty.
Thomas Cowſlad, *Eſq*; 2 *Books.*
John Cowſlad, *Eſq*;
Mr. Curtis, Stamford.

D.

The Rt. Hon. the Counteſs of Dyſart.
George Dodington, *Eſq*;
Mr. Tho. Dawſon, *of* Baſingſtoke.
Miſs Eliz. Dalmon, *of* Baſingſtoke.
Miſs Eliz. Dickens.
Miſs Kitty Dickens.
Rev. Mr. Deane, *Rector of* Woolhampton, Berks.
Rev. Mr. Jonathan Dennis, *Fellow of* Queen's *College*, Oxford.
Rev. Mr. Tho. Clarveato Dockwray, *of* Aldermaſton, Berks.
John Davenport, *Eſq*;
Miſs Sarah Duncombe, *of* Duncombe *Park*, York-ſhire.
Miſs Barbara Duncombe, *of* Ditto.
Mrs. Dotton.
——Dolliff, *Eſq*;
George Drake, *A. M. Fellow of* Baliol *College*, Ox-ford.
Henry Davies, *A. B. Fellow of* Oriel *College*, Ox-ford.
Mr. Dawkins, *Gentleman Commoner of* St. Mary's *Hall*, Oxford.
—— Drake, *A. B. of* St. John's *College*, Oxford.

E.

E.

Sir John Evelyn, *Bart.*
Rev. Mr. Evanſon, *Prebend of* Chicheſter.
Rev. Mr. William Elliott, *Rector of* Hambleton, Surrey.
Mr. Francis Elliot, *of* Godalming, Surrey.
Mr. Evelyn.
Mrs. Evelyn.
Robert Eton, *A. M. of* Jeſus *College*, Oxford, *Eſq*; *Beadle of Phyſick and Arts.*
Robert Edwards, *A. B. Fellow of* Jeſus *College*, Oxford.
Walter Earle, *A. B. of* Oriel *College*, Oxford.

F.

The Hon. Mrs. Finch, *of* Thryberg, Yorkſhire.
Mrs. Jane Fenay, *of* Wakefield.
Mr. Benjamin Foxly.
Mrs. ——
John Frewin, *A. M. Fellow of* Oriel *College*, Oxford.
Rev. Mr. Tho. Fell, *of* Winton *College*.
Samuel Feake, *Eſq*;

G.

The Rt. Hon. the Lady Dorothy Grey.
The Hon. John Grey, *Eſq*;

Mr.

Mr. Harpum Green, *of* Wakefield.

Rev. Jofeph Guibert, *D. D. Rector of* Caterham *in* Surrey.

Mrs. Grubbe, *of* Mitcham *in* Surrey. 3 *Books.*

Mrs. Girdler.

Mr. Benjamin Goodifon, *of* Weftminfter.

Mr. John Gill, *of* Sandall Magna, Yorkfhire.

Mr. Thomas Gill, *of* Wakefield, Yorkfhire, *Gent.*

Miss Goddard.

Mrs. Grogan.

Mr. Philip Garratt, *of* Bafingftoke.

Abraham Gappar, *A. B. of* Oriel *College,* Oxford.

—— Geering, *B. D. Fellow of* Trinity *College,* Oxford. 2 *Books.*

Mr. Jonathan Gardner.

H.

The Rt. Hon. the Earl of Hertford.

Rt. Hon. the Countefs of Hertford.

Rt. Hon. the Lady Dowager Harcourt.

Mrs. Hill.

Richard Hale, *Efq;*

Mr. John Huifh, *of* Chichefter, *Gent.*

Mr. George Huifh, *Town-Clerk of* Portfmouth.

Mr. Thomas Hundefhagen.

William Heberden, *M. D. Fellow of* St. John's *College,* Cambridge.

Rev. George Holcombe, *M. A. of* St. John's *College,* Cambridge.

Mrs. Hawley.

Hugh Hayward, *Efq;*

Chriftopher Hodgfon, *of* Wakefield, *M. D.*

Miss Huggins, *of* Hants. 3 *Books.*

Miss Hunsdon, *of* Shirbourn, Hants.

John Horsefall, *Esq; of* Moss House *in* Craben, Yorkshire. 2 *Books.*

Rev. Mr. Arthur Hele.

Mr. Charles Haddock, *Commoner of* Oriel *College,*
Oxford.

—— Hall, *A. M. Fellow of* Corpus Christi *College,*
Oxford.

Mr. Hall, *Gentleman Commoner of* Corpus Christi
College.

Mr. Philip Hawkins, *Fellow of* Pembroke *College,*
Oxford.

Rev. Dr. Harris, *Fellow of* Winton *College*

I.

Mrs. Ingram, *of* Knottingley *in* Yorkshire.

Rev. Mr. Johnson, *Vicar of* Whaley *in* Lancashire.

Rev. Mr. John Jones, *Curate of* Limpsfield *in* Surrey.

Rev. Charles Jenner, *D. D. Rector of* Buckworth *in*
Huntingdonshire.

Mr. Johnson.

—— Joddrell, *A. M. Fellow of* Trinity *College,* Oxford.

Rev. Eusebius Isham, *D. D. Rector of* Lincoln *College.*

Mrs. Johnson.

Mrs. Barbara Johnson.

Mr. James, Bartholomew Close.

K.

The Hon. the Lady Kay, *of* Grange, *in* Yorkshire.
2 *Books.*

Mrs.

Mrs. Kain.
Mr. Nathaniel Kemp, *Surgeon.*
Mr. Keeling, *Fellow of* St. John's *College,* Oxford.

L.

The Rt. Hon. the Countess of Londonderry.
William Leeves, *of* Tortington, *Esq;*
Miss Lethrellirar.
—— Leeves, *Esq; of* Torton *in* Sussex.
Mr. Harman Leece.
—— Lockwood, *A. B. Fellow of* Oriel *College,* Oxford.
John Robinson Lytton, *Esq;*
Mr. Leech, Staple's Inn.
Mrs. Lilly.
Mr. Edward Lilly.
Mr. Life.

M.

The Rt. Hon. the Lord Middleton.
James Mounsher, *of* Chichester, *Gent.*
Mrs. Machin.
Mrs. Machin, *of* Litchfield-street, St. Anne's.
Mrs. Myers, *of* Mitcham *in* Surrey.
Daniel May, *Esq; of* Suthamsted, Berks. *6 Books.*
Mr. March. *3 Books.*
Miss Mulso.
Mr. Tho. Mulso.
Mrs. Mildmay.
James Merrick, *A. M. Fellow of* Trinity *College,* Oxford. *2 Books.*

—— Mab-

S U B S C R I B E R S.

—— Mabbot, *A. M. of* Pembroke *College*, Oxford.
John Merrick, *M. D. of* Reading, Berks. 6 *Books*.
Matthew Mills, *Esq*;
William Myers, *Esq*; Mitcham.

N.

Rev. Mr. Tho. Nevil, *Minister of* Lingfield *in* Surrey.
George Noyes, *of* Andover *in* Hants, *Esq*;
Mr. John Nicholl, *of* Dyers Buildings *in* Holborn.
Rev. Mr. Cavendish Nevill, *of* Cheet *in* Yorkshire.
  2 *Books*.
Miss Anne Norman.
Miss Mary Norman.
Will. Nowell, *A. M. Fellow of* Oriel *College*, Oxford.
Rev. Mr. Newcome.

O.

General Oglethorpe. 7 *Books*.
Mrs. Oates, *of* Denbigh *in* Yorkshire. 3 *Books*.

P.

The Hon. Charles Powlett, *Esq*;
The Hon. Mrs. Poyntz.
George Pitt, *of* Struffieldsea, *Esq*;
Mrs. Pitt.
Thomas Pitt, *Esq*;
Miss Pitt.
William Pitcairne, *Esq*;
Mrs. Catharine Parker, *of* Shipton *in* Yorkshire.

Rev.

Rev. Mr. George Pigott, *Rector of* Chaldon *in* Surrey.

Rev. John Pearſall, *M. A. of* Pembroke *College*, Oxford.

Mr. Hinkley Phipps, *of* London.

Mrs. Parker, *of* Mitcham *in* Surrey.

Mr. Anthony Pye, *Gent. of* Barnard's Inn, Holborn.

Mr. John Payne, *of* Milford *in* Surrey, *Gent.*

Rev. Mr. Peplar, *Archdeacon of* Richmond *in* Yorkſhire.

Mr. Puckeridge. 4 *Books.*

Mrs. Eliz. Powell, *of* Baſingſtoke.

Rev. Mr. Pearſon, *of* Pamber, Hants.

Rev. Mr. Peck, *Rector of* Ilsfield, Hants.

Mr. Pearſe, *Commoner of* Oriel *College*, Oxford.

William Parker, *A. M. Fellow of* Baliol *College*, Oxford.

Humphrey Parrott, *B. D. Fellow of* Oriel *College*, Oxford. 3 *Books.*

—— Pinnell, *A. M. Fellow of* Corpus Chriſti *College*, Oxford.

—— Peiſly, *A. M. Fellow of* Trinity *College*, Oxford.

John Parfect, *A. B. of* Oriel *College*, Oxford.

R

Thomas Rutherforth, *D. D. Fellow of* St. John's *College*, Cambridge. 2 *Books.*

Mrs. Romer.

Rev. Mr. Edward Pickering Rich, *Rector of* Bagendon, Gloucesterſhire.

Mrs. Hannah Richardſon, *of* Skipton, *Widow.*

Rev. Mr. Henry Richardſon, *of* Thornton, Yorkſhire.

Mrs.

Mrs. Richardson, *of* Chichester.

Richard Richardson, *of* Bierly, Yorkshire, *Esq;*

Mr. William Richardson, *of* London, *Gent.*

Mrs. Richardson, *of* Bloomsbury. 3 *Books.*

Mrs. Rudyerd, *of* Basingstoke, Hants.

Miss Rookes, *of* Dewsbury *in* Yorkshire. 3 *Books.*

Mrs. Frances Russell.

Mrs. Eliz. Russell, *of* Basingstoke, *Widow.*

Mr. John Rogers, *Attorney in* Basingstoke:

Mr. John Russell, *Town-Clerk of* Basingstoke.

Rev. Dr. Russell, *of* Ash *in* Hampshire.

Mr. Lawrence Richardson.

S.

The Rt. Hon. the Lady Georgina Spencer.

Rt. Hon. Lady Sambroke.

Sir John St. Aubyn, *Bart.*

Sir Stukeley Shuckburgh, *of* Shuckburgh, Warwickshire. 12 *Books*

Peter Serle, *Esq;*

Henry Smallman, *Esq;*

Rev. Mr. Spackman, *of* Thackham, Berks.

Mrs. Shipway, *of* Great Billing, Northamptonshire

John Savile, *Esq; of* Methley *in* Yorkshire.

Mrs. Barbara Slingsby.

—— Smith, *of* Heath, *Esq;*

Mrs. Smith, *of* Heath.

Mrs. Smith, *of* Wakefield, *Widow.*

Mrs. Hannah Smith.

Mrs. Sergison, *of* Wakefield.

Mrs. Sarah Smith.

Mr. John Silvester Smith, *of* Newland *in* Yorkshire.

Rev.

Rev. Mr. Sturdy, *Vicar of* Pontefract *in* Yorkshire.

Rev. Mr. John Scott, *Fellow of* St. John's *College*, Cambridge.

Mr. Stead.

John Seyliard, *Esq; of* Pendhill *in* Surrey.

Mr. Stephens, *Surgeon, in* Chancery Lane.

William Smith, *Esq; of* Droxford, Hants.

Rev. Mr. William Smith, *of* Burnham Westgate *in* Norfolk.

Rev. Mr. Sanderson, *of* Bramley, Hants.

Powlett St. John, *Esq;*

Rev. Mr. St. John, *of* Finchamstead, Hants.

John Stock, *A. B. of* Exeter *College*, Oxford.

John Saunders, *A. B. of* Oriel *College*, Oxford.

John Skeeler, *A. M. Fellow of* Oriel *College*, Oxford.

John Sandford, *A. B. Fellow of* All Souls *College*, Oxford.

Charles Stone, *A. B. Demi of* Magdalen *College*, Oxford.

Mr. Swanne, *Fellow of* Magdalen *College*, Oxford.

Mr. Sandford, *A. B. of* Trinity *College*, Oxford.

Mr. Sandys, *of* Trinity *College*, Oxford.

—— Smith, *A. B. of* Trinity *College*, Oxford.

Richard Synes, *Esq; of* Trinity *College*, Oxford.

—— Severy, *A. B. of* Baliol *College*, Oxford.

—— Smyth, *of* Baliol *College*, Oxford.

Rev. Mr. Stockwell.

Rev. Mr. Scott, *Fellow of* Winton *College*.

Mrs. Stevens, *at the Boarding-School at* Salisbury. 30 *Books*.

Miss Hellen Stevens, *in the Close at* Salisbury.

John Archer Shish, *Esq;*

T. *The*

3

T.

The Hon. Lady Tempeſt, *of* Tong *in* Yorkſhire.
John Turner, *Eſq*; *of* Dewſbury *in* Yorkſhire. 10
 Books.
Dr. Thomas.
Rev. Mr. Tol₁, *of* Grewill, Hants.
Rev. Mr. Frederick Toll, *of* Upton Grey, Hants.
Mrs. Tate, *of* Mitcham *in* Surrey.
Mr. Randolph Tutte, *of* Chicheſter, *Gent.*
Miſs Thornton, *of* Wakefield.
Nicholas Tempeſt, *Eſq*; *of* Tong.
Rev. Mr. Rob. Tempeſt, *of* Sheffield.
Rev. William Thompſon, *M. A. Fellow of* Queen's
 College, Oxford.
Rev. Mr. John Thomas, *Rector of* St. Peter's Cornhill.
Thomas Thomas, *A. M. of* Jeſus *College,* Oxford.
Robert Tench, *A. B. of* Jeſus *College,* Oxford.
—— Thomas, *A. B. of* Wadham *College,* Oxford.
Francis John Tyſſen, *Eſq*;

U.

Mrs. Anne Upton.
Rev. Mr. Uvedale.

W.

The Rt. Hon. the Lady Warwick.
Rt. Hon. the Counteſs of Wemyſs.
The Hon. John Ward, *of* Oriel *College,* Oxford.
 The

The Hon. *Mrs.* Walter. 2 *Books.*

Sir William Wentworth, *Bart. of* Britton Hall, Yorkshire.

Sir Thomas Whitmore, *Bart.*

Rev. Mr. Woodyer, *of* Lassam, Hants.

Tho. Worseley, *Esq; Gentleman Commoner of* Corpus Christi *College,* Oxford.

Mrs. Wither, *of* Hall, Hants.

Mrs. Worseley, *of* Hall, Hants.

Miss Wither, *of* Hall.

Miss Walter, *of* Cuckfield *in* Sussex.

Richard Williamson, *Esq;*

Rev. Mr. Washbourne.

Mrs. Wyatt.

Miss Wyatt.

William Wright, *Esq; of* Cheshire.

Rev. Peter Whalley, *B. D. Fellow of* St. John Baptist *College,* Oxford.

Mr. Robert Story Walker, *of* Westminster.

Mrs. Williams, *at* Fryars, Chichester.

Henry Weston, *of* Chertsey, *Esq;*

—— Withers, *of* Carshalton, *Esq;*

Charles Whiting, *B. D. Fellow of* Oriel *College,* Oxford.

John Wylde, *A. B. of* Oriel *College,* Oxford.

Mr. Wickham, *Scholar of* Corpus Christi *College,* Oxford.

—— Winder, *B. D. Fellow of* Trinity *College,* Oxford.

—— Wilmot, *A. B. of* Trinity *College,* Oxford.

Mr. Whorwood, *of* Trinity *College,* Oxford.

Edward Wheeler, *Esq; of* Warwick.

Abel

SUBSCRIBERS.

Abel Walter, *Esq*; 3 *Books*.
Mr. John Walter.
Miss Anne Walter.
Mrs. Wynn, Bedford Row.

Y.

Mr. Young.
Mr. Young, *of* Marlborough.
Rev. Dr. Young, *of* Wellyn *in* Hertfordshire.

Z.

Rev. Mr. Zouch, *of* Sandall Magna *in* Yorkshire.

POEMS

ON

SEVERAL OCCASIONS.

An EPISTLE *to Dr*. YOUNG,
upon his Poem on the Laſt Day.

NOW let the *Atheiſt* tremble; Thou alone
Canſt bid his conſcious Heart the *Godhead* own.

Whom ſhalt Thou not reform? O thou haſt ſeen,

How God deſcends to judge the Souls of Men.

Thou heard'ſt the Sentence how the Guilty mourn,

Driv'n out from GOD, and never muſt return!

Yet

Yet more, behold ten thouſand Thunders fall,

And ſudden Vengeance wrap the flaming Ball:

When Nature ſunk, when ev'ry Bolt was hurl'd,

Thou ſaw'ſt the boundleſs Ruins of the World.

When guilty *Sodom* felt the burning Rain,

And Sulphur fell on the devoted Plain;

The *Patriarch* thus the fiery Tempeſt paſt,

With pious Horror view'd the deſert Waſte;

The reſtleſs Smoke ſtill wav'd its Curls around,

For ever riſing from the glowing Ground.

But tell me, Oh! what heav'nly Pleaſure tell,

To think ſo greatly, and deſcribe ſo well!

How

How waſt thou pleas'd the wond'rous Theme to try,

And find the Thought of Man could riſe ſo high?

Beyond this World the Labour to purſue,

And open all Eternity to View?

But thou art beſt delighted to rehearſe

Heav'n's holy Dictates in exalted Verſe:

O thou haſt Pow'r the harden'd Heart to warm,

To grieve, to raiſe, to terrify, to charm;

To fix the Soul on GOD; to teach the Mind

To know the Dignity of Human-kind;

By ſtricter Rules well-govern'd Life to ſcan,

And practiſe o'er the Angel in the Man.

An

An EPISTLE *to Dr.* GUIBBONS, *a celebrated Physician.*

TO trace all-wondrous Nature's latent Ways,

To meet her Author in each various Maze,

To eafe, to chear, to ftrengthen, to reftore,

For this GOD granted firft the Healing Pow'r;

Important Truft! to Thee fecurely giv'n,

Preferving Man as Delegate of Heav'n.

There are —— but all their Actions how unbleft!

Who deaf to Truth on Second Caufes reft;

And boldly carelefs of their Maker's Will,

Attempt, impoverifh, boaft, infure, and kill;

Not fo haft Thou deny'd Almighty Power,

But verft in Knowledge own'ft a GOD the more;

Hence

1

Hence is thy Patient fearlefs of the Grave,

For Learning and Devotion join to fave:

O *Guibbons!* from whofe Prefence Death retreats,

And on whofe Dictates Health obfequious waits,

How art thou pleas'd, thro' every crowded Street,

The living Proofs of pious Care to meet;

Old Age forgetting its Decays to view,

And Youth improv'd in all its Bloom by You.

Thy Skill would make us on this World be fixt,

But that thy Life reminds us of the next:

Happy, yet loofe to all Engagements here,

Refign'd to God, religioufly fevere!

Induftrious ev'n the meaneft to regard,

Like Guardian Angels kind without Reward.

Garth

Garth vainly ſtrove to blaſt thy riſing Fame,

Which greater * *Dryden* conſecrates to Fame ;

Regardleſs Thou of either Muſe's Lays,

Nor ſtung with Scorn, nor ſtudious Thou of Praiſe.

Yet deign to hear the Wiſhes that I bring,

Unus'd to flatter, and unſkill'd to ſing,

O live ! thou public Bleſſing to Mankind,

In Thee may *Galen*'s Art and Age be join'd ;

Late may thy Buſt ſome hallow'd Dome adorn,

And thine own *Oxford* late her Patron mourn.

'Tis juſt that He who bids us ſtay below,

Should be Himſelf detain'd amidſt Us too.

* In his Tranſlation of *Perſius,* and other Parts of his Works.

M A M-

MAMMON's *PLEA:*

A TALE.

——Melius furto cunctatur & hærens
Ufque alium ex alio fpectando prævidet ictum
Sæpe illum ex longo——
     Vidæ Hieronymi Scacchia Ludus.

M ANY feeming weak Acts by Contrivance
    are done,

Thus at firft the Field's left that the Day may be won.

Old *Turenne*, to diforder the Foe would turn Tail,

Make a Feint, fuffer Lofs, face about, and prevail.

So *Hermes* at Chefs (fays a * Prelate of Fame)

Thought the lofing a Man would be getting a Game.

But to come to the Point. Old Parables tell

A remarkable Inftance that happen'd in Hell:

    * *Vida.*
   B 4   Grim

Grim *Satan* one Night us'd his Spirits like Slaves,

On Pretence that in *England* they ferv'd him by

  Halves:

" Where's *Mammon?* I order you out from the Reft,

" Go, tempt and fecure old Sir *John* of the Weft:

" You have known better Things than beguiling in

  " vain,

" So without Him ne'er think of returning again."

  Well, away went the Fiend, and nine Days he was

  gone,

Then came back to his Mafter; —— but not with Sir

  John:

Satan, mad as he was but to think himfelf fhamm'd,

Roar'd, redden'd, fpoke broken, fhook, fweated, and

  damn'd.

Poor

Poor *Mammon* ſtood up to be heard in his Place,

And thus in plain Terms repreſented the Caſe:

" Let it never be ſaid that you'll hear but one Side,

" Crimes ſuſpected are Crimes till the Criminal's
      " try'd;

" I have ſtay'd, and have let your Knight go; but
      " the Fact is,

" A Parſon ſecur'd both his Faith and his Practice:

" Yet the Int'reſt of all our good Friends here below

" Is as well carry'd on, as the Sequel may ſhow.

" When Sir *John* would not yield, his Attention to
      " draw,

" I appear'd like an honeſt Attorney at Law;

" Then I multiply'd Viſits the more he grew ill,

" Till, *In Nomine Domini* I made his Will.

" It was now the right Time my whole Scheme

" to perform,

" So thus I addreſt my Teſtator in Form:

" Foraſmuch as your Lands are in Charity giv'n,

" To remain ſo while you are rewarded in Heav'n,

" Be this your chief Care, that the Poor be ne'er

" cheated,

" Lord! by how many Ways good Deſigns are de-

" feated!

" 'Tis a Comfort to me in this reprobate Age,

" To ſee Piety thus your Affection engage!

" Now Sir *John* I act always you know undiſguis'd,

" Only beg you in Matters of Law be advis'd,

" The

" The Conveyance is All—Gifts are loſt by Degrees,

" Where the Donors deviſe their Eſtates to Fe'ffees;

" Single Men may forget their own Deaths to ſupply,

" But a legal Town-Corporate never can die;

" Corporations are Guardians, Truſtees, and Directors,

" Of Funds, and of Schools, and Alms-houſes, and

   " Lectures:

" Now whereas you have ſpecify'd theſe in your Will,

" Are not large Bodies beſt, large Deſigns to fulfil?

" Should not Men of Authority manage your Lands?

" 'Tis a Credit to leave one's Affairs in ſuch Hands;

" Let your Gifts be on Magiſtrates ſettled in Truſt,

" Thoſe that puniſh Injuſtice can ne'er be unjuſt:

" Their own Shops will be all Magazines for your

   " Poor,

" Trade and Charity Both may be further'd the more.

        " Chuſe

" Chufe a Town then whofe Juftices yearly are

" fworn;

" What d'ye think of the Place where your Honour

" was born?

" He approv'd, fign'd, and dy'd"——Here the Mo-

narch of Hell

Grinn'd a ghaftly, broad Smile, and fwore——" 'Tis

" all well——

" For inftead of one Knight, to our Share now will

" fall,

" May'r, Aldermen, Burgeffes, Town-clerk, and All."

R E-

RETIREMENT:

An ODE.

I.

ON Beds of Daisies idly laid,
   The Willow waving o'er my Head,

Now Morning on the bending Stem,

Hangs the round, and glittering Gem,

Lull'd by the Lapse of yonder Spring,

Of Nature's various Charms I sing :

Ambition, Pride, and Pomp adieu !

For what has *Joy* to do with You ?

II.

  Joy, rose-lipt Dryad loves to dwell

In sunny Field, or mossy Cell,

Delights

Delights on echoing Hills to hear

The Reaper's Song, or lowing Steer;

Or view with tenfold Plenty spread

The crowded Corn-field, blooming Mead;

While Beauty, Health, and Innocence

Tranſport the Eye, the Soul, the Senſe.

III.

Not freſco'd Roofs, not Beds of State,

Not Guards that round a Monarch wait,

Not Crowds of Flatterers can ſcare

From loftieſt Courts intruding Care:

Midſt Odours, Splendors, Banquets, Wine,

While Minſtrels ſound, while Tapers ſhine,

In Sable ſtole ſad *Care* will come,

And darken the gay Drawing-room.

IV

IV.

Nymphs of the Groves, in green array'd,

Conduct me to your thickest Shade,

Deep in the Bosom of the Vale,

Where haunts the lonesome Nightingale ;

Where *Contemplation*, Maid divine,

Leans against some aged Pine,

Wrapt in stedfast Thought profound,

Her Eyes fixt stedfast on the Ground.

V.

O Virtue's Nurse! retired Queen,

By Saints alone and Hermits seen,

Beyond vain Mortals' Wishes wise,

Teach me *St. James*'s to despise ;

For what are crowded Courts, but Schools

For Fops, or Hospitals for Fools?

Where

Where Slaves and Madmen, Young and Old,

Meet to adore some Calf of Gold.

OF THE

Universal Love *of* Pleasure.

To a Friend.

ALL human Race, from *China* to *Peru.*

Pleasure, howe'er disguis'd by Art, pursue ;

In various Habits this fair Idol dress,

Yet still adore her, still her Power confess ;

She leads pale Hermits to the mossy Cell,

And to the Box the Fop-encircled Bellè ;

The Shape of Business, nay of Virtue takes,

Presides alike o'er Aldermen and Rakes ;

Admirers boasts in every various Rank,

Sends some to Bagnios, others to the Bank ;

Now

Now dwells in lofty Domes and trophy'd Halls,

Now near dark Woods and pensive Water-falls;

One, as she prompts loves Hounds and foamy Steeds,

And lonely One, by midnight Taper reads:

Who build or plan, or dress with Finery smit,

Or rhyme and starve, self-sacrific'd to Wit;

Who heap or scatter Gold, the Grave, the Gay,

Bend to this Monarch's universal Sway.

'Twas hence rough * *Charles* rush'd forth to ruthless

      War.

Hence rov'd to foreign Climes the Patriot-Czar;

Nor found more Bliss to civilize Mankind,

Than *Cynthia* in her new-bought *Chintz* can find.

What home-felt Joys in *Curio*'s Bosom rise,

Glow in his Cheeks, and sparkle in his Eyes?

      * Of *Sweden*.

    C   Is

Is his Wife dead? Or have his Tenants found
Large Heaps of bury'd Treasure in his Ground?
Alas! you guess in vain; from *India* brought,
The Sage a curious Cockle-shell has bought.

'Tis said, the peevish *Lesbia* lately smil'd:
What had her Sullenness of Soul beguil'd?
Some thought Success at Hazard charm'd her Mind,
Or that her favourite Footman had been kind;
Or that her Dog or Parrot had been prais'd——
A new-invented Wash these Raptures rais'd.

To different Objects different Souls incline,
One clips his Hedges; one seeks Whist and Wine;
Rurelia feeds her Hens, and daily churns;
Her Sister such unpolish'd Creatures scorns:

Her

Her Mind is fill'd with Coaches, Cards, and Plate,

Romance, Routes, Operas, Vapours, Chocolate.

When bold *Columbus* took his vent'rous Way,

On the rough Billows of an unknown Sea,

First found the curling Smoke from Hills arise,

And Rocks return the Sailors joyful Cries;

Felt not the Chief such Raptures thrill his Soul,

As *Flavia*, when she wins a doubtful *Vole*.

You, *Decius*, too, from common Frailties free,

A favourite Pleasure feel midst your Philosophy:

For You, beyond the vulgar Joys of Sense,

Enjoy unlimited Benevolence!

To

To a certain Voluminous Scribler.

FORBEAR the Public to abuse,

   With Treatise after Treatise;

Remember how poor *Blackmore*'s Muse

   Dy'd of a Diabetes.

AN INVOCATION
TO A
WATER-NYMPH.

FAIR pearl crown'd Nymph, whose gushing
      Torrent laves

This marble Rock with hollow-tinkling Waves;

Who wont'st in secret Solitude to dwell,

On coral Beds beneath thy Sapphire Cell;

Whose Virgin-Pow'r can break the magic Charm,

Whose Look the black Enchanter's Hand disarm;

Whom Swains in neighb'ring Vales to sing delight,

Kind Guardian of their Flocks from blasting Sprite;

Permit me, Goddess, from thy silver Lake,

With cooling Draught my glowing Thirst to slake!

So,

So, when thou bath'ft, may no rude Satyr's Eye,

From fome deep Brake thy naked Beauties fpy:

May no chill Blaft the ivied Oak invade,

That o'er thy Cavern waves his folemn Shade.

A N

A N
ELEGY *on an* INFANT.

COME, Shepherds, on this Grave your Flourets fpread,

Hantonia's Hope the little *Alcon*'s dead :

I faw ftern Death his cruel Mandate bring,

And heard the Raven clap his fatal Wing;

Thrice at dead Midnight fhriek'd the Owl aloud,

While dim then wav'd a vifionary Shroud.

Hence in deep Grotts, and twilight Shades along

The weeping Wood-nymphs figh a forrowing Song :

The fad Napëans tear their golden Locks,

Lone Eccho wand'ring on fequefter'd Rocks,

By mournful Paufes fpeaks the pitying Tale,

" *Alcon* is dead——lament, each Hill and Dale!"——

So

So *Mysia*'s melancholy Mountains mourn'd,

And *Hylas* loft the Meads and Woods return'd:

Slow crept *Ascanius* with a plaintive Tone,

In Confort murm'ring to *Alcides*' Moan.

Bring then meek Daifies, and the Primrofe pale,

The fnow-clad Lilly of the Velvet Vale,

The purple Violet's Bell empearl'd with Dew,

Cropt at cold Ev'ning, fit on Graves to ftrew:

Be here no gaudy Pink, or Panfy gay,

No Rofe, the Pride of *Venus*, and of *May*;

No full Carnation, deck'd with thoufand Dies,

Like that embroider'd Bow that copes the Skies;

Thefe may fair *Myra* at her Bofom wear,

Or mix them fragrant in her flowing Hair:

No ſuch approach this ſadly-ſolemn Scene,

Or ſpotted Gold, or blended Blue with Green.

Here caſt your Off'rings down, the Turf to grace,

And nine Times round his Grave full ſlowly pace!

Yet ſhould theſe Flow'rs, like *Alcon* ſhortliv'd, fade,

Call the kind Red-breaſt from his ſecret Shade,

With loaded Bill green Myrtle-ſprigs to bring,

And fondly hov'ring plaintive Dirges ſing;

Or bid thoſe Doves that o'er young *Horace* ſpread

Freſh Bays and Buds to ſhield his beauteous Head,

Hither with cooing Elegies repair;

This Babe's as ſprightly, innocent, and fair:

And——but Fate call'd him to eternal Reſt,

A favouring Muſe had warm'd his little Breaſt.

Poor,

Poor, hapless Babe ! —— yet art thou early flown,

The World's vain Vice, unpractis'd and unknown :

The Frauds that lurk beneath a dimpled Smile,

The oily Speech of panegyric Guile ;

The Atheist's Scoffs, the midnight Revels lewd,

Mean Follies of the Beau, Coquette, and Prude ;

The Miser's Care to heap, the Heirs to spend,

The murder'd Brother, and the treach'rous Friend ;

The Statesman's Crafts, the good Man's weary Toils,

The Villain's Triumphs, the stern Tyrant's Spoils :

Far from these Cares, where Breasts seraphic glow,

Thou calmly view'st the noisy Scenes below.

So from some lofty Rock beholds the Swain

The stormy Tumults of the swelling Main ;

Here,

Here, o'er the foamy Floods the wild Winds sweep,

There, sinks the found'ring Vessel in the Deep:

He, while the billowy Surge beneath him breaks,

In Safety listens to the distant Shrieks.

A

C H O R U S,

Translated from the Hecuba *of* Euripides.

I.

SOFT, southern Gale, whose whisp'ring Breath

Skims lightly o'er the curling Wave,

O whither, in this hapless Bark,

Wilt thou convey a weeping Slave?

II.

To *Doria*'s wood-invested Land,

Or *Phthia*'s Pastures shall I go,

Where Father of Field-fat'ning Floods

Apidanus shall hear my Woe?

III.

III.

Or sent to *Athens*, shall I weave

In Tissue Robes the Queen of War ;

    Her polish'd Helm, and Gorgon-shield,

Her foaming Steeds, and glitt'ring Car?

IV.

Or haply in the Piece shall stand

The *Titan*'s Heav'n-defying Crew,

    Whom *Jove*, his Prowess to display,

With angry livid Lightnings flew.

V.

O my lost Children, Parents, Friends!

O *Ilion* smoking on the Plains!

    O my poor Self, whom foreign Hands

Shall bind in curst, disgraceful Chains!

Hereafter

Hereafter in Englifh Metre enfueth
A Paraphrafe on the Holie Book
entituled Leviticus Chap. XI.
Verf. **1**3, &c. Fafhioned after
the Maniere of Maifter Geoffery
Chaucer in his Affemblie of
Foules:

*Containing the Reafons of the feveral Pro-
hibïtions.*

O F feathred Foules, that fanne the buckfom
    Aire,

Not All alike weare made for Foode to Men;

For, Thefe Thou fhalt not eat, doth God declare,

Twice tenne Their Nombre, and their Flefhe unclene:

Fyrft the Great Eagle, ¹ Byrde of feigned Jove,

Which ² Thebanes worfhippe, and Diviners love:

---

¹ Vid. Natal. Com. de Mytholog. Lib. 2. Cap. de Jove.
² Vid. Diodor. Sicul. Lib. 1.

Next Offifrage, and Ofpray, (Both [3] One kinde)

Of Luxurie, and Rapine, Emblems mete,

That haunte the Shores, the choiceft Preye to finde,

And braft the Bones, and fcoope the Marrowe fwete:

The Vulture, void of Delicace, and Feare,

Who fpareth not the pale dede Man to tear:

The tall-built Swann, faire Type of Pride confeft;

The Pelicane, whofe Sons are nurft with Bloode,

[4] Forbidd to Man! —— She ftabbeth deep hir Breaft,

Self Murthereffe through Fondnefs to hir Broode:

They too that raunge the thirftie Wildes emong,

The [5] Oftryches, unthoughtful of thir Yonge:

The

[3] Vid. Patr. in loc.   [4] Vid. paffim in Pentat. & in Ep ad Heb.   [5] *The Night-Hawk is the Male Oftrich, according to Bochart, and the Owl the Female: Here the Author chufes to put both Sexes together. It is remarkable, that in the Hebrew Language*

The Raven ominous, (As Gentiles holde)

What Time She croaketh hoarfely *A la Morte*;

The Hawke, Aerial Hunter, fwift, and bolde,

In Feates of Mifchief trayned for Difporte;

The vocale Cuckowe, of the Faulcon Race,

Obfcene Intruder in hir Neighbor's Place:

The Owle demure, who loveth not the Lighte,

(Ill Semblance She of Wifdome to the Greeke)

The fmalleft Fouls dradd Foe, the Coward Kite,

And the ftill Herne, arrefting Fifhes meeke;

The glutton Cormorante, of fullen Moode:

Regardyng no Diftinction in hir Foode.

guage there are no particular Words to diftinguifh the Sexes of this Bird as there are for the Male and Female Eagle and Raven, &c. The unnatural Quality here affign'd to the Oftrich, is very elegantly mention'd in Job, cap. 39. ver. 16.

The

The [6] Storke, whiche dwelleth on the Fir tree-topp,

And trufteth that no Pow'er fhall Hir difmaye,

As Kinges on thir high Stations place thir Hope,

Nor wift that [7] there be higher farr than Theye:

The gay [8] Gier-Eagle, beautifull to viewe,

Bearyng within a Savage Herte untrewe:

The [9] Ibis whome in Egypte *Ifrael* found,

Fell Byrd! That livyng Serpents con digeft;

The crefted Lapwynge, wailing fhrille Arounde,

Sollicitous, with noe Contentment bleft:

Laft the foul [10] Batt, of Byrde, and Beaft fyrft bredde,

Flittyng, with littel leathren Sailes difpredde.

---

[6] Pfal. 104. 17.   [7] Ecclef. 5. 8.   [8] Gypaetos
is *faid to partake of the Colours as well as the Qualities of the Eagle
and Vulture.* Vid. Gefner.   [9] *So called according to the*
Vulg. Lat. *But in our* Eng. Bib. *The Great Owl.*   [10] Arift.
de Animal. Lib. 4. cap. 13.

To

To Her MAJESTY

Queen *CAROLINE*,

ON HER

ACCESSION to the THRONE:

Being the concluding Copy in the Oxford *Collection upon that Occasion.*

A N *English* Muse shall close the solemn Scene,

  Duteous to celebrate An *English Queen;*

For such is *She,* who by Affection reigns,

And holds our willing Hearts in easy Chains;

Whom partial *Wales Their* Patroness would call,

Tho' to All equal, tho' rever'd by All.

Who makes the *Mitred Prelacy* her Care,

To learned *Wake* (as late to *Smalridge*) dear:

          Yet

Yet shines, on ev'ry meanest Subject, bright,

Chearfully bounteous—Like (God's Gift) *The Light.*

Thee Holy Truth, Thee decent Zeal supports,

Humble in Greatness, and devout in Courts;

Whose faithful Heart not *Roman* Arts could gain,

And Cæsar offer'd Half the Globe in vain.

No such Refusal could *Elisa* boast

When gay *Alanzon* on her wond'ring Coast

His *Lillies* spread:——Irresolute she turn'd,

(Not as when *Mulciber Minerva* scorn'd)

Then said (or seem'd to say) with faint Disguise,

I view all Princes with untempted Eyes.

Far more Sincere, more Pious to refuse,

More Prudent *You,* more Elegant to chuse!

O doubly

O doubly bleſs'd! who, with *Great George*'s Heir,

    Heav'n's richeſt Gifts, Earth's choiceſt Joys may

        prove,

Whilſt (amiable in Majeſty) *You* ſhare

    One Hope, one Faith, one Happineſs, one Love.

Janus well-pleas'd will turn his younger Face

To view the future Glories of your Race;

Britannia happy, in each God-like Son,

And Daughters ruling Nations, not our Own;

Extenſive Good! which *You*, with gen'rous Care,

For This, for other Lands, and diſtant Days prepare:

Hence, glorious on *Thy Self* reflected ſhine

The dawning Virtues of Thy *Num'rous Line*,

By *Thy* Example form'd, taught by *Thy* Skill divine.

All Factions hence—(for All *thy* Worth confeſs)

The *Queen*, the *Mother*, and the *Chriſtian* bleſs.

                                           O

O CAROLINE! for ev'ry Grace renown'd,

With Wit, with Judgment, and with Beauty crown'd,

Deign to accept This Tribute of my Praise,

Tho' rude of Stile, and artless be the Lays:

Our youthful Bards, on *Isis'* Banks retir'd,

Unseen in Courts, by Swains alone admir'd,

(Such once was *Addison*—whom *You* inspir'd.

As yet but hear how *Foreign Muses* please,

With *Spanish* Grandeur, or with *Tuscan* Ease;

But, when the *Living Languages* they know,

(A Gift, which we to *Royal Bounty* owe)

Each rising Genius shall more boldly soar,

Sweetly disclosing Charms unknown before;

Our *Athens* then, more various in Her Songs,

Like *Fame*, will praise Thee with a Hundred

      Tongues.

          S

So the rough Agates, in their native Mine,

Or lay conceal'd, or only faintly ſhine,

'Till ſome kind Hand, diſtinguiſhing their Worth,

Calls all their Multitude of Beauties forth;

Then Nature's mimic Gems (improv'd by Art)
        ſurprize,

And Rocks, and Clouds, and Trees, in little Landſkips
        riſe.

AN

O D E

ON THE

P A S S I O N.

I.

IN Sable clad, *Urania* come,

    Dictate a Pity-moving Lay,

Such as may paint a dying GOD,

    And all his Wounds and Pangs display:

What Time the blissful Saints above,

Struck with his Suff'rings and his Love,

    Began to heave unusual Sighs;

Each Seraph tore his Palmy-crown,

Each threw his Harp or Trumpet down,

    And Grief a while usurp'd the Skies.

II.

II.

But hark! I hear triumphant Shouts,

    Of *Jews* that dare infult their Lord;

At whofe Approach pale Sicknefs fled,

    Madnefs and Storms obey'd his Word:

This gracious Benefactor fee,

Stretch'd out in Anguifh on the Tree!

    How deep the Traces of the Scourge!

      His bending Head how pale!

    The Spear has gor'd his fnowy Side,

      His tender Feet the Nail!

III.

Sudden the Graves their dreary Depths difclofe,

    Low, doleful Sounds run murm'ring thro' the Air;

The fhrouded Bodies from the Charnels rofe,

    And gliding by, their trembling Kindred fcare;

                  The

The twifting Rocks their fulph'rous Beds difplay'd,

   Earth's deep Foundations to the Center fhook;

The Sun was cover'd with a ten-fold Shade,

   Unable on Meffiah's Pains to look:

Remoteft Lands the dreadful Portents felt,

And, for a Time, in Wonder, Fear, and Darknefs

     dwelt.

IV.

Beneath, lo! *Mary* weeping ftands,

  In Tears moft pitifully fair,

And beats the Breaft, where *Chrift* had hung,

  And tears her long difhevell'd Hair——

" Where can I lay my mournful Head?

" My Son, my King, my God is dead!

  " To gloomy Deferts let me go,

" Among the horrid Rocks and Woods,

" The Caves, and penfive-falling Floods,

  " Indulging Solitude and Woe!"——   V.

V.

And shall not vile, ungrateful Man,

Bear in these Griefs a wretched Part

Roll in the Dust, and beat his Face,

Bleed in his Bowels, and his Heart?

While stern *Repentance* near him stands,

Pointing to Heav n with meagre Hands!

O let us weep, and humbly pray,

That Faith no longer mourn,

That Peace may raise her oliv'd Head,

And Righteousness return.

.VI.

Then Pride no more shall swell her purple Crest,

Or mad Ambition kindle lawless Strife ;

Pale Envy then shall leave the tortur'd Breast,

And frowning Murder break his reeking Knife ;

I

Old

Old Avarice his Heaps of Gold forego,

 Sly Theft no more the Traveller beguile,

Luſt ſhall grow whiter than the new-fall'n Snow,

 And Rage be calm'd, and Malice learn to ſmile:

Ev'n *Satan*'s Self ſhall feel a heavier Chain,

And gnaſh his Teeth, and ſhake his burning Spear

   in vain.
       VII.

Alas! far other Scenes appear,

 Man ſtill enſlav'd to tenfold Guilt,

Toſt on from Vanity to Vice,

 Forgets his Saviour's Blood was ſpilt:

Forgets he left the Realms of Day,

Changing his glorious Robes for Clay:

 With inexpreſſive Mercy fill'd,

His Angels left, and Em'rald Throne,

Deigning as Mortal to come down,

 To be deſpis'd, forſaken, kill'd.   VIII.

VIII.

Yet there remains a dreadful Day,

 When, after Years in Follies fpent,

This vain, fantaftic World fhall fall,

 With ev'ry melting Element.

Methinks I hear the Angel—" Come—

" This Trumpet calls ye to your Doom."—

 The fimple *Indian* ftarts amaz'd,

  The *Jew* now dreads the Rod,

 Curs'd is the Koran by the *Turk*,

  The Atheift owns a God.

IX.

Down rides Meffiah on the Wings of Wind,

 His fiery Sword of Juftice blazing round;

To Vengeance comes He, yet with Mercy kind,

 Satan and Death behind his Chariot bound.

O turn we from the burning Sinner's Pains,

   His agonizing Struggles, piercing Plaints;

And let us liften to the rapt'rous Strains,

   Sung by the Juft, the Seraphs, and the Saints:

How for Mankind the filial Godhead bled,

And proud Captivity an humbled Captive led!

The Eighth ODE of the Second Book of HORACE.

To BARINE.

1. ULLA si Juris tibi pejerati

      Pœna, Barine, nocuisset unquam,

Dente si nigro fieres, vel uno

        Turpior Ungui,

Crederem.———

2. ——— Sed tu, simul obligâsti

Perfidum Votis Caput, enitescis

          Pulchrior

Imitated.

To Sir ROBERT WALPOLE.

1. IF ever Juftice with her iron Hand,

    Had dar'd to thruft thee from this groaning

    Land,

Or on thy Front, t' avenge a People's Cry,

Burnt the red Marks of fhamelefs Villany;

Or, as from righteous *Japhet*, cropt an Ear,

Which, daily, fine-fpun Flatt'ry wont to hear;

Poor *Britain* might appeafe her Griefs, and fmile,

And hope her Genius had not left her Ifle.

2. But You——the lefs your Country you befriend,

The more the Courtier-mob before you bend:

                Each

Pulchrior multo, Juvenumque prodis

Publica Cura.

3. Expedit Matris Cineres opertos

Fallere, & toto taciturna Noctis

Signa cum Cœlo, gelidâque Divos

Morte carentes.

4. Ridet hoc (inquam) Venus ipsa, rident

Simplices Nymphæ, ferus & Cupido,

Semper ardentes acuens Sagittas

Cote Cruentâ.

5. Adde

Each vile Corruption lures 'em to your Purse,

As hungry Insects a corrupted Corse;

While bowing Bards with panegyric Lays,

Wipe off, or turn your Vices to your Praise;

As if the Muse, with all her *Pindus'* Stream,

Cou'd wash a Negro white, or clean your Name.

3. What tho' you swear your Country to redress,

To shield in War, to cherish her in Peace;

None dare thy false, *Ligurian* Words believe,

Who deem'st it Depth of Wisdom to deceive.

4. At this Corruption smiles with ghastly Grin,

Foretelling Triumphs to her Sister Sin;

Who, as with baneful Wings aloft she flies,

" This ruin'd Land be mine "——exulting cries;

E   Grim

5. Adde quòd Pubes tibi crescit omnis;

Servitus crescit nova; nec priores

Impiæ tectum dominæ relinquunt

Sæpe minati.

6. Te suis Matres metuunt Juvencis,

Te senes parci, miseræque nuper

Virgines

Grim Tyranny attends her on her Way,

And whets his flaming Sword that thirſts to ſlay.

5. How widely ſpreads thy Pow'r! almighty
Knight!

Conqueſt is ſurer when you bribe, than fight:

No more let *Perſia* hail her laurell'd Lord,

Before a Seſterce what avails a Sword?

Yet ſure 'tis ſtrange your Slaves will Slaves remain,

Tho' ten Times kick'd they come, they cringe again;

As fooliſh *Phædria* ſtill ſigh'd for his Whore,

Tho' the dear Jilt had thruſt him from her Door.

6. Striking her Breaſt, what Tears has Virtue
ſhed,

To ſee plain Juſtice, Truth, and Valour fled?

Who

Virgines nuptæ, tua ne retardet

Aura Maritos.

Who can relate her home-felt, Patriot-Pains,

How much ſhe ſighs, how deeply ſhe complains,

That *Britain* bends to thy corruptive Pow'r,

Debauch'd. like *Danäe*. with a golden Show'r?

Carmen

Carmen in celeberrimi Gloveri LEONIDAM.

VOS animæ illuſtres, quæ jam per amœna vireta

Elyſiii, ad liquidos fontes divina piorum

Concilia heroûm celebratis, & horrida longe

Tartara deſpicitis, tetras caligine ſedes;

Leönidâ invicte, & Dithyrambi dia Juventus,

Diomedonque, & vos vix tanti nominis umbræ,

Ouæ ſimul ob patriam cecidiſtis vulnera paſſæ;

Reſpicite & vatem, qui veſtris tanta triumphis

Dona parat Muſarum, intactaque nomina verſu

Aonas in montes, Pindique cacumina duxit,

Scilicet ille novus acies, nova caſtra camœnâ

Suſcipit audaci; en quantis late obſtrepit arvis

Agminibus

Agminibus Xerxes, inftructoque undique campos

Marte tenet, fpoliifque hoftes Orientis onuftos

Barbaricis, variifque armis, vafto crdine pandit.

Contrà **Argiva Phalanx,** haud magnis freta catervis.

Sed propriâ virtute valentior, agmine pauco

Obfidet Oetëas fauces; anguftaque circùm

Caftra tenet, quà faxa altis horrentia fylvis

Defupèr, & fructæ nemorofa cacumina rupis

Immanem obtendunt umbram; dum per juga fumma

(Præruptas fedes,) tranquilla filentia latè

Servat opaca quies, & amantes afpera Nymphæ

Aërii montis fylveftria templa tuentur.

Inftat ovans Xerxes, adverfaque prælia mifcet:

Sed quid tot gentes, quò tanta fuperbia belli!

Quas ibi tunc ferro ftrages, quæ funera fparfit

Leonidas, clarifque infigniit arva tropæis!

Viribus

Viribus haud æquis, haud diis concurritur æquis.

Scilicet Hos cingi monuit fulgentibus armis,

Vox vigilis patriæ, anguftifque invicta periclis

Libertus acrem incuffit per pectora flammam.

Quin parvo confueta cohors vovêre juventam

Virtuti Martique : injecta catena magiftri

Hos fævi invitos peregrina ad prælia traxit,

Et patriâ avulfit, natifque & conjuge dulci

Pacatifque arvis, longoque errore coëgit

Perque vices cœli varias, perque afpera Ponti,

Haud cædis cupidos, animifve hoftilibus actos

Regna ignota fequi, atque aliena laceffere bella.

Vis tanta imperii, nimiique licentia fceptri !

Qui verò mentes arrectus percipit ardor

Dum canit immemorem Lethive horæve propinque

Fervere

Fervere Leönidam, certæque occurrere morti.

Fortunate Heros, cui candida fata dederûnt

Pro patriâ periiffe tuâ! felicior ergo

Tu forti Æneâ, & cedet damnatus iniquâ

Sorte tibi Thefeus, ipfoque Alcide tropæa,

Tu majora refers: utcunque domaverit anguem

Ille ferum, & Nemeâ vaftum fub rupe leonem;

Olli haud pro patriâ licuit labente perire,

Haud tantî tot Gefta, & duri mille labores.

Vos pariterque uno devincti vulnere amoris,

Ducitis antiquæ tranquilla oblivia curæ,

Quæ jam frondenti per opaca cubilia myrto,

Tu *Teribaze* ingens, *Arianæ* que umbra fidelis,

Refpicite & faltem, fecretâ e fede, poetam

Profequitur cineres tanto qui munere veftras,

Qui

Qui manibus gratis tam pulchros fpargere flores

(Trifte minifterium) veftram dignatur in urnam,

Ipfe pias etiam exequias, & ferta pararem,

Quin felix tumulus partoque infignis honore

Haud ultrà ornari geftit, ftudiique recufat

Dona fupervacui, & levioris munera mufæ.

At faltèm liceat duram miferefcere fortem

Amborum, & lacrymâ triftem donare favillam.

Vos autem Ætei rupes, & grandia faxa,

Et nemorum quæcunque umbræ juga lata coronant,

Vos veteres pinus, & tactæ fulmine quercus

Cum Nymphis falvete! & tu formido verendi

Relligiofa loci, quà folo in littore fecum

Heroûm (ut perhibent) fimulacra ingentia paftor

Sæpe fub obfcurum noctis volitare pavefcit.

2   Tu

Tu Glovere fimul, feu publica fortè miniftras

Munera, civiles agitans in pectore curas,

Seu dulces numeros divinaque carmina pangas

Mufarum fuavi per mentem inftinctus amore,

Tuque etiam falve! neque enim fibi vendicat omnes

Jam lauros *Milto*, fiquas ferat *Anglia* Mater;

Non Britonum folus frontem velâffe coronâ

Pieriâ, aut liquidam libâffe Aganippida jactat,

Tantâ utcunque lyrâ primævi fata parentis,

Tartarëafque domos fonet, & cœleftia Bella.

A S-

ASTROPHIL to his SON, aged Seven Months.

O THOU! with whom I fondly share

My faithful *Stella*'s Love, and Care,

To thee 'tis giv'n to tumble o'er

Thy absent Sire's poëtic Store,

(With eager Hands these Lines to seize

And tear, or lose 'em, as you please,)

Thou too from Pedantry art free,

And I can safely sing to thee.

What tho' thy Age no Skill can boast,

In one small Round of Follies lost;

Yet ev'n thy Toys, and Tears, and Strife,

Act all the World in little Life.

3   Alike

Alike Man aims at all he can,

And Imitation teaches Man:

—But then has Man his Play-things too?—

—Yes fure.—Amufements all allow,

And are more ferious Fools—than thou.

We differ, only in th' Intent

As idle—but lefs innocent.

PHILANDER,

AN

Imitation of *SPENCER:*

Occasioned by the Death of Mr. WILLIAM
LEVINZ, *of* M. *C.* OXON, NOV. 1706.

" To You alone I sing this mournful Verse—

" Made not to please the living, but the Dead—

" To You, whose soft'n'd hearts it may empierse

" With Dolours—(if you covet It to read—

    " And if in You found pittie ever place,

    " May You be mov'd to pittie such a case.

SPENCER.

ON THE
DEATH
OF
Mr. *WILLIAM LEVINZ*.

Purpureos spargam flores, animamque Philandri
*His saltèm accumulem donis, & fungar inani
Munere*————   VIRG. Æn. VI.

G IVE me, ye weeping Nine, the softest Airs,

  Whilst I with you *Philander*'s Fate condole;

Let Pity grace each sadly-pleasing Verse,

And tender Words that thrill the melting Soul:

  Echo shall kindly answer as I mourn,

  And gently-wafted Sounds my doleful Plaints

   return.

F   When

When rural *Spencer* fung, the lift'ning Swains

Wou'd oft' forget to feed the fleecy Throng;

    The fleecy Throng, charm'd with the melting

        Strains,

Fed not—but on the Mufick of his Song;

    His *Mulla* would in ling'ring Bubbles play,

    'Till his pleas'd Waters ftole unwillingly away.

    And cou d my Verfe but with its Theme com-

        pare,

Moving as *Spencer* I my Grief wou'd tell;

    The ravifh'd Bard fhou'd to *Elyfium* hear

A fecond *Colin* mourn a fecond *Aftrophel*.

    My Lays fhou'd more than equal Glory boaft,

    And the fam'd *Mulla* be in fmoother *Cherwell* loft.

I

                        Cherwell !

Cherwell! blefs'd Stream while thy *Philander* liv'd!

Where-e'er thy Waves in mazy Windings turn,

    Tell ev'ry Stream of whom they are depriv'd,

And bid 'em all in fobbing Murmurs mourn :

    Oft' on thy Banks he'd tell thy Praifes o'er,

    Twas there I faw him laft——but oh! fhall fee no

        more.

    Look, faid the Youth, (as then he wond'ring ftood)

How *Cherwell*'s Waves in dinted Dimples fmile!

    I joy to fee his amicable Flood

With circling Arms embrace the happy Soil :

    How loth he feems thefe charming Shades to

        leave,

    That from his filver Urn a nobler Grace receive!——

        ——But

—But mute is now the Muſick of that Voice,

That to th' attentive Flood ſuch Praiſes gave!—

'Mong Bones and Skulls the dear *Philander* lies,

Cold, cold, and ſilent as the diſmal Grave!—

Mourn then, ye Youths, for ever mourn his Fate;

Ye cannot grieve too long—but oh ye grieve too

late!

—Look all around the Woods, and Plains, and

Floods;

Do not ev'n they the mighty Loſs deplore?

Lo Pleaſure leaves the Floods, and Plains, and

Woods!

And penſive Birds now warble there no more;

But pining Doves, and moaning Turtles coo,

And Choirs of Swans make up the Harmony of

Woe.   Their

Their tuneful Sorrow ravishes my Ear,

While mourning Vegetables please the Eye;

    The sick'ning Flow'rs their Heads but faintly rear,

And droop beneath the dewy Tears, and die!

    Like them the Youth a thousand Charms cou'd
        boast,

    —But oh the Youth like them those short-liv'd
        Charms has lost!

Say, You his Friends, Companions of my Woe,

Say what kind Gentleness adorn'd his Mind?

    Tell me, can You such native Candour show?

And may we still a true *Philander* find?

    Vain Hope!—let all with gen'rous Shame confess,

None e'er excell'd you more—and yet cou'd know
        it less.

        F 3   Oft

Oft wou'd the Youth into himſelf deſcend,

And act at once the Confeſſor and Saint;

  How pleas'd he'd ſee th' examin'd Breaſt un-
      ſtain'd,

And ſay with modeſt Joy *I'm Innocent!*

  Confed'rate Graces ſpoke him Whole Divine,

  All beautiful without, and ſpotleſs all within.

  And muſt ſuch fair Perfection yield to Fate?

Why was thy early Goodneſs ripe ſo ſoon?

  Ye Pow'rs! let Virtue have a longer Date,

Or ſome prevailing Muſe to make it known:

  Oh! cou'd theſe Lays proportion'd Praiſes give,

  The lovely Youth ſhou'd ſtill in deathleſs Numbers
      live!

                       Thou

Thou conſtant Object of my lab'ring Thought!

Tho' thy dear Preſence cruel Death denies,

    Oft is thy Shade by kinder *Morpheus* brought,

And oft by Fancy to my longing Eyes:

    Sometimes my Thoughts thy dying Gaſps re-

        new,

    Ev'n now methinks I ſee all Death expos'd to

        View.

    I ſee *Philander* on his Death-bed lain!

What griping Pangs his tortur'd Heart corrode!

    Look how reſign'd he bears each ſmarting Pain!

And inly groaning invocates his God!

    How chang'd he looks! how aſhy pale his Hue!

    I ne'er unwilling ſaw the lovely Youth 'till now!

        Are

Are thoſe the Arms with which we oft embrac'd ?

Thoſe Hands, benumn'd, and cold, are thoſe like his ?

And his dear Lips, by conſtant Learning grac'd,

Say, did they tremble, and look wan as theſe ?——

——Love might with Fear a doubtful Strife main-

        tain,

But that my Griefs preſent a yet more diſmal Scene.

Behold ! his Friends all croud around his Bed !

Hark with what bitter Cries they o'er him moan !

    Look on their ſtreaming Eyes ! what Tears they

        ſhed !

Their Grief makes all his Miſeries their own !

    And while this Pomp of Death *Philander* ſees,

    The dying Youth by their's perceives his Miſeries.

                    Now

Now his chill Face with eager Lips they kiſs,

Graſp his cold Hand, and take their laſt Farewel!—

How languiſhing they fix their Eyes on his!

Their aking Sight cou'd there for ever dwell!

    Too well they know thoſe parting Looks are vain,

    And turn themſelves aſide — yet needs muſt look

        again.

—But doubtful Miſts ſwim hov'ring o'er his Eyes,

That feebly round their hollow Orbits rowl;

    Whilſt in imperfect Groans and leſſ'ning Sighs,

With pious Careleſſneſs he yields his Soul;

    His Soul unfetter'd ſeeks the Realms of Light,

    And to her native Heav'n ſhe takes her tow'ring

        Flight.

                            But

But who can tell his weeping Mother's Care?

His Death in vain by silent Friends is hid.

For conscious Tears the fatal Truth declare,

And their expressive Silence says, He's Dead!

Her still-born Sorrow speaks an inward Woe,

Beyond what Sighs, or Tears, or Words unequal

show.

O cease, thou good *Sophronia*, left forlorn,

For thy much-lov'd *Philander* weep no more;

Those, who thy Son's sad Fate cou'd never mourn,

Will ev'n his living Mother now deplore;

For when such Piety in Tears they view,

Their soften'd Hearts must grieve to sympathize

with You.

Look

Look on thy Daughter, beauteous in Diſtreſs,

Nor think while *Stella* lives *Philander* loſt;

  Oh! may kind Heav'n in Her your Griefs redreſs,

And You in one a num'rous Bleſſing boaſt!

  May His redoubl'd Life to her return!

And you in *Stella* ſee *Philanders* yet unborn!

HIERONYMI FRACASTORII.

AD

JOAN. BAPTISTAM TURRIANUM VERONENSEM.

BATTE, animos quando triftes curafque le-
vare

Mufa poteft, ego nunc fortem, cafufque fupremos

Ipfe meos trifti folabor carmine tecum,

Et tecum dulces natos, quos funus acerbum

Abftulit, æternâ & pariter caligine texit,

Conquerar: ut faltem tenebris & nocte perenni,

Quantum opis eft noftræ, miferorum nomina demam.

Quæ potui, dum vita illos, auræque fovebant,

Exhibui

TO

BAPTISTA TURRIANO,

FROM THE

Latin of FRACASTORIUS:

On the Death of his Sons.

SINCE with sweet Balm the Muse alone can
  heal

Sad Sorrow's Wound, and sooth the troubled Mind,

Listen a While my *Battus,* nor refuse

Her grateful Gift of grief-beguiling Verse;

Which to thy much-lov'd Sons, whom dreary Death

Has wrap'd in *Stygian* Shade, she weeping pays.

At least her Song, if e'er her Song avail'd,

From their fair Names may snatch the Veil of Night.

E'er yet oppress'd by Fate's untimely Stroke

My tender Care inform'd their helpless Age;
      This,

Exhibui genitorque, gubernatorque duorum

Infelix, primas alter vix fingere voces,

Alter adhuc teneris jam tum decerpere ab annis

Prima rudimenta, atque omen præbere parenti.

Quos ego (fed Zephyri fpes portavere paternas)

Cenfueram, fi fata darent, quum pofceret ætas

Fortior, ad dulces tecum traducere Mufas

Affiduos, citharamque humeris fufpendere ebur-
  nam.

Inde ubi jam cœlum, ac Solem, fulgentiaque aftra,

Terramque, & liquidos ignes, æquorque profundum

Mirari inciperent, latifque animalia campis,

Te monftrante viam, te rerum arcana docente,

Mens fuerat dulces Sophiæ deducere ad hortos,

Hortos, quos ver perpetuum, quos aura Favonii

This, yet with lisping Accent scarce could frame

Th' imperfect Word, while This in early Dawn

Cropt the first Flow'rs of Knowledge, and began

To give glad Promise of a fertile Spring.

If Fortune e'er had blest my blooming Hopes

When to firm Manhood grew their ripen'd Age,

My Hand had led them to the mossy Grotts,

Of *Cirrha's* Vale, their Father's much-lov'd Haunts,

And on their Shoulder hung *Euterpe's* Lute.

Thence, when their soaring Minds had trac'd the

   Stars,

The golden Sun, broad Deep, and dædal Globe,

While thy sage Mind disclos'd the dubious Way;

To the fair Gardens of Philosophy

Had bore them wond'ring, which eternal *Spring*

And mild *Favonius* feed with balmy Dews

            Of

Semper alit, semper cœlesti nectare pascit.

Hic tremulo, & longâ confecto ætate parenti

Purpureos legerent flores : seniique levamen,

Threïciâ canerent citharâ, quæ plurima quondam

Audîssent te populeâ meditante sub umbrâ,

Divino mirantem Athesim dum carmine mulces,

Et rerum canis & teneri primordia mundi.

Fortunate senex, si natorum ore referri

Fata sinant, ut nata chao antiquissima rerum

Materies visi correpta cupidine pulchri

Arserit, atque Deûm thalamo complexa jugârit

Corpora prima : quibus discordia nata hymenæis,

Et divisa locis, suprema petiverit ignis

Purior, & nitidis vicinus sederit astris :

Quem

Of Nectar; then to crop purpureal Flowers,

Sweet Solace of their hoary Parent's Age;

Oft too to chear thy pensive Eve of Life

Their skilful Hands had strung the *Thracian* Lyre

To Notes like Thine, that on the daisied Marge

Of *Athesis*, beneath the Poplar Shade,

They heard thee sing, of Nature's infant Dawn,

The wild Wave hushing with thy magic Strain.

O how thine Age, my much lov'd Friend, had smil'd

If e'er thou could'st have heard thy Sons declare,

How Matter first from shapeless Chaös born

With Beauty long'd to joyn; how Discord rose

At length to Texture and to Shape confin'd;

How to th' ethereal Vault the purer Fire

Aspir'd, and to the starry Reign upflew,

G

While

Quem juxta per inane amplum se suderit aër:

Ima autem tellus vasto circum obruta ponto

Constiterit : quam dudum hinc inde agitantibus undis

Substerni late campi, deformiaque arva

Paullatim apparere supra, & concrescere montes

Cœperunt, procul & nudas ostendere cautes,

Mox nemora, & virides undis mirantibus ornos.

Montanis tum speluncis, & rupibus altis

Exsiluere udæ formoso corpore Nymphæ,

In viridi flavos siccantes littore crines.

O fortunatum nimium, si Numina tantum

Hæc mihi servassent, si non casura dedissent.

Verum aliter Lachesi visum est quo tempore primum

Natorum cœpit producere fila duorum :

Quippe auram miseris, & dulcem noscere vitam,

3   Spemque

While Air diffusive fill'd the spacious Void.

How o'er the Globe a Desert waste and wild

Of Sea was roll'd, 'till from the watry Scene

At length emerg'd broad Plains and oozy Fields,

And high to Heav'n the Mountains heav'd their Backs

Horrid with many a Cliff; while cloath'd in Green

Tall Forests from the wondering Waters rose;

And from the rocky Caves and Caverns dank

Sprung forth the Nymphs in naked Beauty bright,

And dry'd their Tresses on the verdant Shore.

O thrice had Fortune blest my blissful Life,

If ne'er the Gods had cropt these blooming Hopes

And kept them still inviolate; but Death

Just when they promis'd in the rising Dawn

Of Infancy so fair a Spring of Flowers,

G 2   With

Spemque fui dederat præbere : alia omnia ventis

Tradita, nocte atrâ & tenebris involverat Orci.

Non licuit firmos annis, viridefque juventâ

Infpicere, & caræ ad metam deducere vitæ.

Nec potui votis, nec ope adjuviffe paternâ

Clamantes, fruftraque patris fuprema petentes

Auxilia, & notâ nequidquam voce vocantes.

Heu mortem invifam ! quis te mihi, Paulle, Deorum

Arripit, & miferum complexibus abftrahit iftis ?

Tu prior immiti correptus morte parentem

Deferis, & dulces auras & lumina linquis.

Quod te fi tali dederant fub lege futurum

Fata mihi, non jam fuerat mœroris abunde ?

Non gemitus ? quid me è tam multis patribus unum,

Cœlicolæ, lacrimifque novis, & morte recenti

Opprimitis, caroque etiam fpoliatis Iulo ?

Heu

With baleful Breath forbad the Bud to bloom,

And buried all beneath the difmal Shade

Of *Tartarus*; nor could my anxious Care

Lead them to glowing Youth, and Manhood firm,

And fee them run the weary Length of Life.

Nor could their Parent's earneft Prayers or Art

Save them, tho' loud they call'd with moving Voice

HIs medicinal Aid!——O cruel Death,

O fay what God, my *Paulus*, ftopt thy Breath,

And tore thee ruthlefs from my cold Embrace?

You firft dear Youth your weeping Father left

No more to view the Beam of chearful Heav'n.

Thy Fate alone had plung'd my lab'ring Soul

In Woe too deep, then wherefore, heav'nly Pow'rs,

Add ye frefh Caufe of Grief, and bid new Tears,

New kindred Tears for fweet *Iülus* flow?

How

Heu miferande puer, quanto plena omnia luctu

Liquifti abfcedens! quem non vefana Deorum

Incufavit inops, quum te complexa jacentem

Afpiceret laniata comas & pectora mater?

Ah misera, ah male faufta parens, quid numina

      fletu

Sollicitas? jacet ille, velut fuccifus aratro

Flos tener, & fruftra non audit tanta gementem.

Ah misera, ah quid fublatum complexa moraris?

Ille tuus non jam eft.   Vos illam in funere, matres,

Collapfam accipite, exanimemque reponite tectis.

  At vos, infontes animæ, cariffima nuper

Pignora (quod mifero fupereft optare parenti)

Semper avete mei, ut licuit, femperque valete.

Seu dulce Elyfium functos, umbræque tenebunt

                    Sanctorum

How thy mad Mother every God accus'd,

As o'er thy Coarſe reclin'd, her Hair ſhe rent,

And beat with pityleſs Hand her bleeding Breaſt.

O ceaſe, fond Mother, to ſollicit thus

The Gods with fruitleſs Cries! as the fair Flower

Whom yet in infant Bloom the ſhining Share

Cuts from the Parent Glebe, *Iülus* lies

Deaf to thy loud Complaints; no more embrace

His clay-cold Limbs with unavailing Arms!

Ev'n now, ſad Follower of his ſable Herſe

She faints—ye Matrons lift the drooping Dame,

Rouſe ſtruggling Life, and bear to ſoft Repoſe!

Ye pure, unſpotted Shades! receive this Hail!

This laſt Adieu, Remembrance of my Love,

And Friendſhip's Pledge ſincere! where'er ye dwell,

Whether ye wander in *Elyſian* Vales,

Or

Sanctorum nemorum, puro seu sidera coelo,

Ipse ego vos semper lacrimis, vos carmine tristi

Prosequar, & vestris persolvam justa sepulchris:

Donec me vobis tenuem conjunxerit umbram

Summa dies, natis æquat quæ sola parentes.

Interea curas numeris, Musàque levemus,

Batte, animos: quando rerum mortalis origo est,

Scilicet & quondam veniet labentibus annis

Illa dies, quum jam curvo sub vomere taurus

Desudet, terramque gravis proscindat arator,

Nunc ubi cæruleæ rostris spumantibus undæ

Sulcantur, verruntque citæ freta longa carinæ.

Nec vos, ô liquidi fontes, æterna manebunt

Sæcula, se tanto quamvis pater efferat amne

Eridanus, tumidusque fluat tot cornibus Ister.

Quin

Or triumph in the Star-befpangled Skies,

Still grateful will I pay the duteous Tear

And Rite of facred Song, nor yearly fail

To crown with frefheft Wreaths your honour'd Urns.

Mean time, my *Battus*, let the Mufe relieve

Our Sorrow-lab'ring Breafts and footh our Cares;

Since All is frail and built on Mortal Bafe.

The Days will come, when at the tardy Plow

The Steer fhall pant, and thro' the ftubborn Mold

The Share fhall pafs, where now the winged Bark

Cleaves the blue Deep, and fkims the glaffy Plain.

Nor fhall the Fountains fam'd in ancient Song

Still ftream exhauftlefs; tho' the mighty *Po*

Devolves fo full a Tide, and *Ifter* laves

Un-

Quin etiam aërii montes, mirabile dictu,

Taygetus, Syphilusque, jugo & Cymbotus opaco

Innumeras post æstates, ac sæcula longa,

Senserunt seniumque suum, supremaque fata;

Ex quo materies thalamos, primosque hymenæos,

Atque elementa novus sensit discordia mundus.

Unnumber'd Channels, with enormous Flood.

The cloud-capt Mountains, proud *Taygetus*,

Tall *Sypilus*, and crown'd with woody Cliffs

Cymbotus, thro' the Course of endless Years

Have from their deep Foundations felt the Force

Of gradual Dissolution and Decay:

Since Matter first embrac'd the smiling Form

Of Order, and the warring Elements

Together rush'd to form th' emerging World.

To the Right Honourable

GEORGE DODINGTON, *Esq*;

AS late I rov'd by *Lodon*'s whispering Stream,

 Studious to sound in Verse thy much-lov'd

Name,

Apollo came, and touch'd my trembling Ear——

" To praise a *Dodington*, rash Bard! forbear!

" What can thy weak, and ill-tun'd Voice avail,

" When on *that* Theme my *Young* and *Thomson*

 " fail?'

O N

MAY MORNING.

To a LADY.

WINTER no more the weeping Fields de-
  forms,

Pours the deep Snow-drift, or defcends in Storms,

But rural Mufic wakes the blithfome *Spring*,

And every Wood invites to love and fing;

See in yon' Bow'r the Goddefs' Self appears,

A Rofe-bud Garland on her Locks fhe wears,

And on her Wrift two cooing Turtles bears:

Join'd Hand in Hand attends her Sifter *May*,

Simple, yet fair; and tho' not wanton, gay;

Behind a Train of Nymphs and Youths advance,

Touch the foft Lute, and join in fprightly Dance.

Hither

Hither ye City-Nymphs and *Belles* repair,

To sport in Freedom, and a purer Air!

Safe may ye wander thro' the cooling Wood,

Or listen to the Birds and falling Flood :

No Beau-Deceivers lurk among the Flocks,

No ruffling Winds shall dislocate your Locks ;

But Peace and Innocence true Pleasures yield,

While new *Vauxhalls* arise in every Field.

But the light Herd of well-bred Dames disdain

The calmer Pleasures of the painted Plain ;

Gay *Flavia* hates a Mead and purling Rill

More than a Church, Small-pox, or Mercer's Bill ;

" For who, she cries, a *London*-Life would change,

" Pensive in solitary Woods to range ;

" To

" To walk without a Beau in some lone Vale,

" Nor *Handel* hear, but the sad Nightingale ;

" Or sit at solemn Whist by gloomy Fires,

" With aukward Parsons, Justices, and Squires?" —

But blest with strong, unfashionable Sense,

You relish rural Ease and Innocence:

Can leave Ridotto's for an useful Book,

Or sit at Plain-work by a murm'ring Brook:

In useful Labours pass each virtuous Day,

Nor sigh for Opera, Masquerade or Play.

What Joy to view from far the sweating Steer,

The Blackbirds or the Milk-maids Song to hear ;

Count budding Cowslips, or with Lambkins play,

Sing with a Nymph, or with a Shepherd stray !

Then

Then caſt thee weary on the painted Ground,

Where Hazels caſt a checquer'd Shade around;

While iſſuing from a Bud a Bee ſhall come,

To bleſs thy Slumbers with a drowſy Hum.

But who can ſleep! ten thouſand Joys combin'd,

Employ the Smell, the Ear, the Eye, the Mind!

Have youthful Poets dreamt of golden Days,

When Fruits ambroſial ripen'd in their Lays,

Did Honey-ſtreams in liquid Numbers flow,

In the rich Verſe ſpontaneous Harveſts glow?

Soon imag'd Charms, and faint Deſcription cloys,

Fancy may paint, but Nature gives the Joys:

Who taught the Nightingale her Neſt to form,

In uſeful Beauty, wonderful and warm?

(May

(May no rough Ruſtic violate the Boughs,

Where hangs her little, moſſy-circled Houſe)

Who ſent the Dam to cull the choiceſt Food,

Now in the Foreſt ſeeking now the Flood,

And to the hungry Young with Haſte convey

The Worm untaſted, or the Inſect-Prey:

Who ſwell'd the Lilly with a pearly Dew,

Who bad gay Earth her radiant Robe renew,

The Stream in Concert with the Linnet run,

And the World ſmile beneath a warmer Sun?

'Tis Nature's Pow'r!—Thy all-benignant Hand

Spreads every Joy, and bleſſes every Land!

Grant, gentle Goddeſs, no corroding Care

In rankling Chains our reſtleſs Hearts enſnare;

H O while

O while around us all is Joy and Peace

Let Sorrow die, let jarring Paffions ceafe;

So fhall Mankind Thy general Praifes fing,

And in their Bofoms feel another Spring.

On a GENTLEMAN *whose Mistress had an ill Breath.*

LOVERS 'tis said are blind—but *Thirsis* shews,

These Sighers lose not Eyes alone, but Nose;

Go, doting Fool—a fragrant Favourite seek,

Nor *Egypt*-like, adore a nauseous Leek.

58990

VERSES

VERSES

ON

HENRY *the Eighth's ſeizing the Ab-bey-Lands, and on Queen* ANNE's *Augmentation of Livings.*

THERE liv'd a Race to good *Chariſſa* dear,

Who rais'd a thouſand Domes devote to

Pray'r;

A thouſand mattin Choirs with White array'd,

In tuneful Tributes all their Vows convey'd;

Then Charity was wont her Iſle to love,

And oft for this to change the Realms above:

But when ſhe hapleſs found fierce Rage begin,

Where Force reform'd but by a pious Sin,

When

When arm'd Devotion would the Prieſt expel,

And Royal Sacrilege was chriſten'd Zeal,

She view'd, ſhe mourn'd, ſhe fled her rifled Iſle,

While ravenous *Henry* gave a Looſe to Spoil.

And now where Towers ſtretch'd far their taper
　　　Shade,

Where hallow'd Walls religious Pomp diſplay'd,

The ſolitary Traveller ſtares around,

Oft halts——oft deems he hears ſome ſcreaming
　　　Sound,

And treads with trembling Knees the conſecrated
　　　Ground.

For oft o'er Graves the Shepherd tends his Herd,

And points where Saints and Martyrs lay interr'd;

H 3　　　　　　　Here

Here in ſtill Deep of Night are Peaſants ſear'd,

When the tall Ghoſts ſtalk ſlow with Steps un-
   heard,

When moaning Cries the loneſome Ruins fill,

So pitiful they howl! and ſhriek ſo hollow ſhrill!

Theſe diſmal Yells the Shepherds ſhiv'ring hear,

And feign bold Talk to chace the freezing Fear;

But when the Nod of ſome much-injur'd Shade

Sadly invites 'em with his beck'ning Head,

They fly. They wonder at their Speed unknown,

Glad that they ſhun the Sprite—yet, haſt'ning on,

Oft look behind to view the Sprite they ſhun.

Where holy Pilgrims wont to kneel and pray,

Now browzing Goats, and lowing Oxen ſtray,

O'er mould'ring Pillars creeps the bluſhing Vine,

And leafy Fig inveſts each ſolemn Shrine,

        O'er

O'er venerable Virgins fculptur'd Heads,

Nods horrid Thorn, and darkfome Elder fpreads,

And with clofe Foliage o'er the pictur'd Walls,

Time's favourite Plant the mournful Ivy crawls;

Warning the Cock, no more the midnight Bell,

Call'd the pale Sifters from the filent Cell,

Whofe Lamps to blefs benighted Wand'rers Sight,

Caft thro' thick Windows a dim doubtful Light.

Religion wept.—to fill fair *Albion*'s Throne,

Till gracious Heav'n fent bounteous *Anna* down;

Alike for Mercy and for War renown'd,

She rais'd the drooping Priefthood from the Ground;

Stoop'd from her Throne to hear each mournful Sigh,

With Thunder in her Hand, but Pity in her Eye;

　　　　　Queen

Queen of th' Afflicted! form'd by Heav'n to melt,

At every Woe distrestful Virtue felt:

Thy Name shall last with freshest Laurels crown'd,

Long as thy *Churchill*'s Sword shall be renown'd;

'Till *Danube* cease to tremble at thy Name,

Forgetful of the Blood that stain'd his fearful Stream.

VERSES

VERSES

Written after seeing Windsor *Castle.*

FROM beauteous *Windsor*'s high and story'd
    Halls,

Where *Edward*'s Chiefs start from the glowing
    Walls,

To my low Cott, from ivory Beds of State,

Pleas'd I return unenvious of the Great.

So the Bee ranges o'er the vary'd Scenes

Of Corn, of Heaths, of Fallows, and of Greens,

Pervades the Thicket, soars above the Hill,

Or murmurs to the Meadows murm'ring Rill;

Now haunts old hollow'd Oaks, deserted Cells,

Now seeks the low Vale-Lilly's silver Bells;

                       Sips

Sips the warm Fragrance of the Greenhouse Bow'rs,

And taftes the Myrtle and the Citron-flow'rs;

At length returning to the wonted Comb,

Prefers to All his little Straw-built Home.

AGAINST

AGAINST
DRESS.

To a LADY.

I.

WHY will *Neæra* fondly deck

With pearly Rows her polish'd Neck;

Why with the feathery Tippet hide,

Her swelling Bosom's spotless Pride?

With genuine Beauties, all your own,

You need not borrow *Venus'* Zone.

II.

Whence all this fashionable Care,

To curl that lovely Length of Hair.

Which Nature meant shou'd flow profuse,

In Ringlets beautifully loose:

The

The ſtudied Fopperies of Art

No real Elegance impart.

III.

Mark, fair One, in its native Bed,

How blooms the Cowſlip's velvet Head;

What luſcious Cluſters load the Vines,

Whoſe Growth no ſkilful Hand confines;

How ſweet the Lark and Nightingale

Untaught and artleſs charm the Vale.

ON

ON

LUXURY.

WHY, ye Profuse, has Nature work'd in vain,

To cloath with useful Woods *Britannia's*

Plain?

Why the stout Oak, great King of Forests, made,

The knotted Ewe, and Beech of solemn Shade?

Why bends the Ash high-rustling o'er the Hills,

Why Poplars tall o'erhang the creeping Rills?

My Lord contemptuous of his Country's Groves,

As foreign Fashions foreign Trees too loves:

" Odious! upon a Walnut-plank to dine!

" No—the red-vein'd *Mohoggony* be mine!

" Each Chest and Chair around my Room that stands,

" Was ship'd thro' dangerous Seas from distant Lands:

3   Death!

" Death! fhou'd your *Britifh* Cloths my Limbs

" infold!

" How clumfily they fett when lac'd with Gold!

" For me rich *Perfia*'s Products crofs the Deep,

" I owe my Drefs to Silkworms, not to Sheep!

" And fent to *China* the poor Sailor burns,

" To fetch me Cups, Bowls, Urinals and Urns."——

While thus the Great to modifh Trifles ftoop,

Each Science forrows, all the Mufes droop;

For thofe who moft fhould patronize the Mufe,

Neglect, or dread, or fetter, or abufe.

Pictura hangs the Head, and fighing ftands,

And drops the ufelefs Pallet from her Hands;

Sculpture that hop'd our lofty Halls to grace,

With *Raleigh*'s, *Bacon*'s, *Milton*'s, *Newton*'s Face,

3   (Names

(Names that from *Britons* claim a loud Applause)

Weeps, breaks her rusty Chissel and withdraws.

   The thoughtless Rich on rosy Beds repose,

With downy-finger'd Sloth their Eyes to close;

The Hand quite unemploy'd, and mute the Tongue,

Like idle Lutes in musty Cases hung:

Man grows fatigu'd with even Paths and plain,

Life sweetest tastes diversify'd with Pain;

The Table-Diamond shines not half so bright,

As brilliant Angles rich with varied Light.

Should Fortune frown, her Favourite's Visions cease,

His Soul starts conscious from the Bands of Ease;

Adversity to Action wakes his Worth,

And gives each hidden Talent, Life and Birth.

So when bleak Winter ſtrips the mournful Trees,

The Traveller, Towns, Temples, *Villa's* ſees,

That in warm Spring inviſible had ſtood,

Too deeply boſom'd in the branching Wood.

O N

W O M E N.

I.

THREE Talents to the Fair belong,

Beauty,. Cunning, and a Tongue;

By which Men lose these other Three,

Reason, Time, and Liberty:

Great is th' Advantage when their Pow'r they try,

In killing those that still desire to die.

II.

What triple Panoply, my Friend,

From Beauty's Darts can Souls defend?

Tho' sullen *Satan* never lov'd,

Yet this unlucky Truth he prov'd,

I   That

That Man by Woman might be manag'd beſt,

He ruin'd *Eve,* ſo left to her the reſt.

III.

Yet, partial Muſe, forbear to blame

The Fair for this increaſing Flame;

Each Lover is their eaſy Prey,

And thoſe who will be Captives may:

The Loſs is ſure that with Deſire is ſought,

We know the Snare, yet labour to be caught.

IV.

No Wonder then old *Mico*'s Breaſt,

At Sixty-five is ſtill poſſeſt;

Cupid in Time grows paſt Controul,

Enthron'd within our inmoſt Soul;

For Love's a Charm that ne'er can be undone,

While thus th' Inchanted raſhly help it on.

A N

A N

O D E,

Written in a Grotto near Farnham *in* Surry, *call'd* LUDLOW'S Cave.

I.

CLOSE in this deep Retreat
O coolly let me sit,

Shelter'd from the sultry Day!

Sirius and *Sol* with burning Beams

So strike the gasping Fields below,

That not an Ox is heard to low,

Or little Warbler from his Throat

To pour the sweetly-winding Note.

II.

II.

The Nymphs that keep this circling Wood,

And beauteous *Naïads* of the neighb'ring Flood,

With their Dew-dropping Hair,

Oft to this unadorned Cave repair,

To dance and trip it in a Round

On the smooth and hallow'd Ground ;

And say—" That *Dian*'s Grott, and *Thetis*' Bow'rs,

" Must yield in Coolness and in Shade to our's."—

III.

'Twas Here, as old Traditions tell,

A wither'd Witch was wont to dwell ;

The magic Mutterings of whose Voice could call

A thousand Dæmons from their darksome Hall,

Bid haste the wild Winds from their Northern Caves,

Obscure the Moon, and rouse the roaring Waves :

Here

Here Lud, retiring from fierce Battle came,

And from his Helmet quaff'd the cooling Stream;

Leant on his Spear, unrein'd his foamy Steed,

To pasture on the green, refreshful Mead.

IV.

Here what a solemn Silence reigns,

Save the Tinklings of a Rill,

That gushing from the hollow Hill,

Pensive, as it runs, complains.

But hark! methinks a Spirit speaks,

A Voice from the remotest Caverns breaks;——

" From the vain World learn, Mortal, to retire,

" With true Ambition to high Heav'n aspire;

" Grandeur and Glory trifling Hearts trepan,

" These Toys disdain, for Virtue makes the Man."——

I 3 V.

V.

Let me therefore ever dwell,

In this twilight, folemn Cell,

For mufing Melancholy made,

Whofe Entrance venerable Oaks o'erfhade,

And whofe Roof that lowly bends,

With awful Gloom my ferious Thoughts befriends:

Here let me dwell,

'Till Death fhall fay——" Thy Cavern leave,

" Change it for a darker Grave."

TO A
FRIEND,
On his MARRIAGE.

WHEN *Peleus* wedded on *Theſſalia's* Plain,

The ſilver-footed Regent of the Main,

The Gods came flocking to the Nuptial Feaſt,

Each left his Nectar to be *Peleus'* Gueſt;

Jove laid his Scepter and his Thunders by,

In Amber Clouds deſcending from the Sky;

While *Juno* ſat all-blooming by his Side,

With Charms like thoſe which for the Apple vy'd;

Next, gayly-dancing, Hand in Hand there came,

The Vine-crown'd Youth, and Laughter-loving

Dame;

Nor abſent was the Trident-bearing God,

In Coral Chariot o'er the Waves he rode,

Bad the fierce Whirlwinds in their Caverns ſleep,

And Calmneſs ſmile upon the glaſſy Deep;

Laſt came, prepar'd the Bridal Joys to tell,

Each green-rob'd Nereïd with her chorded Shell:

A Band of heav'nly Virtues, far more bright

Than fabled Gods, to grace this Pair delight;

Faith, pure-ey'd Nymph in ſnow-white Robes ar-
    ray'd,

Meek *Modeſty* of every Eye afraid;

Honour with manly Front erect, appears,

Hymen, an ever-blazing Torch who bears,

And *Love* great God of Raptures——not the Boy

Who blindly wont to favour guilty Joy,

But

But who prefiding o'er chafte Marriage-Hours,

All the foft Luxury of Fondnefs pours,

While no harfh Jars the mutual Blifs controul,

But Wifh meets Wifh, and Soul cements to Soul.

Hail, happy Pair! may ne'er your Pleafures ceafe,

May heart-felt Paffion with your Years increafe!

  Go, trifling Wits, infipidly deride

The conftant Hufband, and the tender Bride;

Rail at the real Blifs ye never knew,

Grow impotent and rotten in a Stew.

THE

THE

SONG of *JUDITH*,

Paraphras'd from the APOCRYPHA.

BEGIN the Song! to GOD the Timbrels strike,
Tune a new Psalm, and let *Jehovah*'s Name
Dreadfully glorious, from the Chorus burst
In full harmonious Majesty of Praise!

The Warrior's Prowess, and the Battle's Rage
GOD breaks and withers; his almighty Arm,
Shield, of the Righteous, in black Midnight's Shade,
In Safety led me thro' surrounding Hosts.

Assyria from the North her People pour'd
Lords of the rugged Mountains; Armies fraught

With

With Thousands and ten Thousands, as they pass'd,

Hid the high Hills, and stopt the Torrent-Floods.

  Where are the Boasts of Vengeance, Spoils, and

    Deaths!

What-time they long'd to see my blooming Fields,

Smoak under Volumes of the fiercest Flames

In sad Illumination ; and to tear

The wondering Infant from the Mother's Breast

Hush'd into soft Repose, and on the Stones

Dash pityless : in vain they wish'd to tread

On mangled Youths, from the fond Husband's Side

Snatch the young Bride, and mad with lawless Lust

To make the violated Virgin shriek :

For lo ! th' almighty Lord in Glory thron'd,

Girded with Strength, hath shewn his matchless Pow'r,
I

       And

And deign'd to send a weak Vicegerent forth,

To cruſh their Inſolence.   No youthful Hoſt,

Or towering *Titan*'s Sons, with brawny Arms,

And Strength unquell'd, no Giant-Warrior ſtrode

To the rough Combat, but a tender Maid

The ſoft-ey'd *Judith*, with her beauteous Form

O'ercame the rugged Hero, nor could Rage

Unmelted ſtand the Lightning of her Eye!

'Twas then unmindful of her private Grief,

When *Iſrael* mourn'd, the Widow's ſable Garb

She caſt away, and with the choiceſt Oils

Her Limbs anointed, call'd forth every Smile,

And every latent Grace, in Order bound

The braided Ringlets of her golden Hair,

Deckt in the brighteſt Robe her Form, and ſhone

In

In all the Charms of Nature and of Art.

How did the captivated Hero gaze

At every matchless Feature, gaz'd and figh'd

By Turns, and own'd that all his Soul was Love!

That Inftant in her Hands the Faulchion grafp'd

The female Warriour, and vigorous Stroke

Sever'd the haughty Satrap's Head. The *Mede*

At this aftonied ftood, the *Perfian* Bands

In fearful Wonder afk; What GOD unfeen

Such Pow'r beftow'd, and fteel'd a Woman's Heart.

Not fo revenging *Ifrael*—ev'ry Child

Of Sorrow ftarts into unufual Shouts

Of Joy and Gratulation. *Affur* bears

The fearful Tidings thro' his weeping Camp,

And trembles: But victorious *Ifrael* cries,

" *Purfue, Purfue!*"——The Lord in Battle ftrong

Nerv'd

Nerv'd every Arm, and urg'd the vigorous Hoſt,

Till ſudden Death o'ertook the *Painim* Bands

Diſcomfited and fal'n, and all the Plains

Float with Effuſions of *Aſſyrian* Blood.

Hence will I praiſe my GOD! high-thron'd in
  Heav'n,

Invincible in Strength and Pow'r; who ſaid,

Let all Things be,—and all Things were.—Whoſe
  Touch

The Mountains and the Waters fly; whoſe Breath

Melts the hard Rock like Wax! yet ev'n this GOD

So great and glorious, deigns to bend his Ear,

To liſten to the meek Man's Pray'r, and joins

Mercy with Terror, Tenderneſs with Pow'r.

What

What Off'rings can we pay to such a GOD,

What Incense can ascend to Heav'n, or Lamb

Be worthily accepted! yet an Heart

Pure and unspotted will the Lord receive

Well-pleas'd, and wrap it in eternal Peace.

But Wo! to those who meditating Wrongs

And Violence to *Israel*, slay her Sons

Or spoil her Lands: *Jehovah*'s Self shall come

At the last vengeful Judgment, and shall say

Before his dread Tribunal——Hence to Hell

Ye Grinders of my People, there to feel

Th' undying Worm, to mourn, to toss, to yell,

Roll'd in a Deluge of sulphureous Flame!

A

A

PARAPHRASE

On the 65th Psalm.

TO Thee, *Jehovah*, grateful *Sion* sings,

And with thy Praise thy holy City rings;

To Thee, from Heav'n O pitifully bow,

Mankind prefers an universal Vow!

The Snares of Sin against my Soul prevail,

A contrite Spirit let thy Mercy heal!

Blest is the spotless Man who dwells with Thee,

The Treasures of thy Temple shall he see,

Be wrapt in Bliss, and in thy own Abode,

Enjoy the fullest Glories of his God.

What Wonders shall the Lord of Sabaoth shew,

The great Salvation of the World below!

Who

Who with his Strength the Lands in Safety keeps,

And all that see his Wonders in the Deeps,

Faſt the Foundations of the Mountains joins,

And girds about with Pow'r his mighty Loins!

He ſpeaks—the Tumults of the People ceaſe—

He nods—the raging Ocean ſinks to Peace—

Thy Tokens dart Amazement to the Soul,

And all the Nations fear from Pole to Pole!

Thee with a fiercer or a fainter Ray,

The Morn and Evening praiſe, the Night and Day!—

GOD from his copious Rivers Plenty pours,

Cloaths the luxuriant Earth with balmy Flow'rs,

Bathes in ſoft genial Dews the tender Root,

And loads the gladſome Year with golden Fruit;

K   From

From vernal Skies abundant Bounty ſends,

And luſcious Fatneſs from his Clouds deſcends;

Hence fragrant Greens the pathleſs Wild o'erſpread,

For Joy the little Hills exalt their Head,

The crowded Folds with num'rous Bleats reſound,

And the full Valleys laugh and ſing and ſhout around.

STANZAS,

STANZAS,

Imitated from PSALM CXIX.

I.

SAY, how shall thoughtless, easy-natur'd Youth,

   Be pure from all the Stains their Follies give?

  O let them learn the sober Law of Truth,

Know thy Rewards, and answerably live.

II.

  Full of this Hope I seek thee, dearest Lord,

And left the Foe once more my Soul should win,

   Deep in my Heart I treasure up thy Word,

A constant Guard against the Charms of Sin.

III.

III.

How am I pleas'd when Joy, and Faith, and Awe,

Strive which fhall moft employ my various Tongue,

That loves to dwell on All thy wond'rous Law,

Guide of my Life, and Subject of my Song!

IV.

Now Fame or Pleafure, or the wealthy Eaft,

May tempt indeed—but never fhall remove,

The lively Zeal that burns within my Breaft,

Thy Name to honour, and thy Law to love.

O D E.

O D E.

I.

TO tinkling Brooks, to twilight Shades,
　　To defert Profpects, rough and rude,
With youthful Rapture firft I ran,
　Enamour'd of fweet Solitude.

II.

On Beauty next I wond'ring gaz'd,
　Too foon my fupple Heart was caught;
An Eye, a Breaft, a Lip, a Shape,
　Was all I talk'd of, all I thought.

K 3　　　　　　　　　III.

III.

Next, by the ſmiling Muſes led,

 On *Pindus* laurell'd Top I dream,

Talk with old Bards, and liſtening hear

 The Warbles of th' inchanting Stream.

IV.

Then, *Harmony* and *Picture* came

 Twin-nymphs my Senſe to entertain,

By Turns my Eye, my Ear was caught,

 With *Raphael*'s Stroke and *Handel*'s Strain.

V.

At laſt, ſuch various Pleaſures prov'd,

 All cloying, vain, unmanly found,

Sweet for a Time as Morning-Dew,

 Yet Parents of ſome painful Wound;

             VI.

VI.

Humbly I afk'd great *Wifdom*'s Aid

  To true Delight to lead my Feet ;

When thus the Goddefs whifpering faid,

  " Virtue alone is Blifs compleat."

         Written

Written in a Lady's WATCH-CASE.

I.

BEauteous Machine! let Love thy Movements
    guide,

Whilst envy'd thou shalt grace *Aurelia*'s Side !

'Tis thine to please each Hour—a Task how great !

Which *Cupid* thus instructs thee to compleat.

II.

When the Nymph kindly mourns her Shepherd
    gone,

Whirl all thy little Wheels, and urge them swiftly on :

The Nymph deceiv'd with thy officious Haste,

Shall smile to see that Time can fly so fast.

III.

But at the Swain's Return O slack thy Pace,

And slowly linger round thy figur'd Race :

I

She

She ne'er can deem too ſhort the Shepherd's Stay,

When, like great *Juno*, thou ſhalt lengthen out the

Day.

IV.

So mayſt Thou ſooth her Woes, her Joys improve,

Thy ſelf directed by the God of Love;

And *Beaux* and *Belles* with Wonder ſhall declare,

That *Cupid nicks* with nicer Art than *Quare*.

O N

ON A

BEAUTY *with ill Qualities.*

I.

MISTAKEN Nature here has join'd
A beauteous Face and ugly Mind;

In vain the faultlefs Features ftrike,

When Soul and Body are unlike;

Pity, thofe fnowy Breafts fhould hide,

Deceit, and Avarice, and Pride.

II.

So in rich Jars from *China* brought,

With glowing Colours gayly wrought,

Oft-times the fubtle Spider dwells,

With fecret Venom bloated fwells,

Weaves all his fatal Nets within,

As unfufpected, as unfeen.

AN

A N

AMERICAN LOVE-ODE.

Taken from the Second Volume of Montagne's
Essays.

I.

STAY, stay, thou lovely, fearful Snake,

    Nor hide thee in yon darksome Brake:

But let me oft thy Charms review,

Thy glittering Scales, and golden Hue;

From these a Chaplet shall be wove,

To grace the Youth I dearest love.

II.

  Then Ages hence, when thou no more,

Shalt creep along the sunny Shore,

Thy

Thy copy'd Beauties ſhall be ſeen ;

Thy Red and Azure mix'd with Green,

In mimic Folds thou ſhalt diſplay :——

Stay, lovely, fearful Adder ſtay.

THE

THE

Second EPODE of *HORACE* imitated.

HAPPY the Man who free from Cares and
       Strife,

(Such was the calm primæval State of Life)

Securely ploughs his Fields and ancient Seat,

Fix'd in th' Indulgence of propitious Fate:

Him nor loud Trumpet's Clangors rouse to Arms,

Nor the fierce Deep's tempestuous Rage alarms;

He shuns the Bar, the Pride and empty State

That gilds the glittering Palace of the Great.

Now, pleasing Toil, the wanton-wreathing Vines

In soft Embraces to the Poplar joins;

To prune his barren Boughs his Hand employs;

Or distant-bleating Herds with silent Joys

His

His ravisht Eye contemplates, wand'ring wide

On a green Valley's wood-incircled Side.

From his prest Combs fat Streams ambrosial flow,

While fleecy Flocks their useful Pride bestow.

When ripe *Autumnus* blushes in the Fields,

Crown'd with the Fruits his own Luxuriance yields,

What Joys he feels to pluck the pendant Pear,

Nurst with his own kind Hand's assiduous Care !

Or purple, livid Grapes, the sweet Reward

Of old *Sylvanus*, his gay Garden's Guard

Beneath yon' Oak's impenetrable Shade,

On Mantle green of the Mosaïc Mead,

His languid Limbs he shelters from the Heat,

While Nightingales their luscious Lays repeat :

And the shrill Brook in Nature's Concert flows,

That courts and lulls the Soul to soft Repose :

But

But when the Rage of Tyrant-Winter low'rs

Big with tumultuous Winds, and frozen Show'rs,

He rushes to the Chace with sprightly Hounds,

While the fierce Boar his Spear impetuous Wounds;

Or careful spreads his Net, delusive Lure,

The greedy Thrush unheedful to secure:

Or captivates the Crane, or timorous Hares,

Or Engines for the Felon-Fox prepares.

These mild Amusements calm the troubled Breast,

Parents of Mirth and Health, Content and Rest.

Mean while her destin'd Part the Wife employs,

Wreath'd in th' Embraces of her blooming Boys;

Chaste as a *Sabine*, or *Appulian* Dame;

She wraps aspiring Piles in chearful Flame;

With fondling Smiles receives her weary Spouse,

For whom she spread her Feasts, and deck'd her

House: Then

Then milky Streams from swelling Dugs are roll'd

That Herds afford within th' incircling Fold;

From fragrant Casks rich Wines profusely flow,

And with domestic Cheer an easy Feast bestow.

Nor me the Turbott or the Scarr delight,

Nor Oysters, fair *Lucrina*'s Pride, invite,

Whom Winter's Fury to *Italia*'s Main

Drives loudly thund'ring on the stormy Plain;

Nor the plump Partridge, soft voluptuous Bait,

Or Quails that swell the Banquets of the Great,

Than turgid Olives more allure my Taste,

Whose Boughs with fat Profusion bend opprest;

Or loosening Mallows' salutary Juice,

Or Sorrel sweet, that lowly Meads produce,

Or rescued from the Wolf a play-full Lamb;

(Tho' much I grieve to hear the plaintive Dam.)

Amidst

Amidst this Luxury, what sweet Delight

To watch the joyful Flocks Return at Night!

To see the weary Oxen's lowing Train,

Whose languid Necks th' inverted Plow sustain,

And Swains that swarm around the glossy Hearth,

In Innocence of Joy and rural Mirth.

L   A

A

PARAPHRASE

ON THE

13th ODE of the 3d BOOK of
HORACE:

Address'd to Miss Oglethorpes. 1705.

I.

WHILE *Sol* with thee, dear Fountain,
plays,

O stay and listen to thy Praise!

Then stealing soft with silver Flight,

Outshine the polish'd Crystal's beamy Light.

II.

Yon' sunny Mountain's richest Wine,

Shall mix his noble Juice with thine,

Each

Each Bowl shall with those Flow'rs be crown'd

Whose Blossoms blow thy beauteous Banks around.

III.

The young Kid too that *Flavia* loves,

That harmless o'er her Grotto roves,

That Kid which her fair Fingers feed,

A spotless Victim to thy Stream shall bleed.

IV.

His budding Horns in Shoots appear,

The Promises of Love and War,

In vain! the Wanton's glowing Blood

With purple Streaks shall marble all the Flood.

V.

Thy Coolness chears the wither'd Plain,

And *Sirius* burns the Field in vain;

When

When Beasts in Moans, expressive, grieve,

Thy frigid Waves the pining Herds relieve.

VI.

Lambs dance around thy bubbling Urn,

And whiter from thy Flood return,

There Birds their feathery Beauties see,

And sing and dress their painted Plumes by Thee.

VII.

Look, how this Oak, itself a Grove,

Lifts high his hundred Arms above;

How thick the tufted Moss below,

Thro' which thy prattling Waters fall and flow!

VIII.

O Nymphs, tho' I unequal sing,

Yet thus adorn'd this humble Spring,

With noblest Fountains ranks its Name,

While You reign each a Naïad of the Stream.

A

A

FRAGMENT *of a* SATIRE.

SHALL essenc'd Coxcombs who from Toilettes
   come,

Strut, and squeak Nonsense in the Drawing-room,

Sagacious Critics of a Knot or Fan,

Soft *Sporus's*, faint Images of Man,

All form'd of Nature's tend'rest, Porcelain Stuff,

Their snowy Fingers shelter'd by the Muff,

Heroes for Sonnets, but unfit for Fights,

Herds of emasculated *Sybarites*,

Shall painted Insects, busy buzzing Things,

In Armies rise and Favour gain from Kings?

While wounded Veterans obscurely mourn,

And S——r sees Lawrels from his Temples torn?

O courtly *Atticus*, my Warmth you blame,

Unconfcious of the glowing Patriot's Flame:

I feel, I feel, its kindling Raptures rowl,

From Pleafures and from Bufinefs fteal my Soul,

And while it ftrongly in my Bofom beats,

No more I rove collecting claffic Sweets,

Nor warlike *Homer*'s well-fought Battles warm,

Nor Fairy Forefts of wild *Spenfer* charm ;

No more I weep while awful *Tragedy*

Like *Sophocles* array'd comes ftalking by,

(Leading ill-fated *Oedipus* the Blind,

Or the lame * Wretch in defert drear confin'd)

Nor in mild *Maro*'s Groves and Grotts rejoice,

Nor *Doric* † Shepherd's fweetly fimple Voice,

* *Philoctetes.*   † *Theocritus.*

No

No more convey'd by *Pindar*'s rapid Song,

I see great *Theron*'s Car victorious whirl along,

Nor crown'd with Grapes with gay *Anacreon* laid

Beneath a Plantane praise some beauteous Maid,

But oft resounding in my trembling Ear,

Methinks my Country's dying Groans I hear.

    Rise, Satire, rise; 'tis sinful to be mute:

The Muse should whirl a Dart, not tune a Lute;

Gigantic Vice, beyond huge *Tityus*' Size,

Enormous Growth! o'er half *Britannia* lies;

O let my Satire on its Vitals feast,

Like the fierce Eagle on that *Tityus*' Breast!

    Yet Oh! what Hero Folly can confound?

The dull, lethargic Villain feels no Wound:

L 4   Culprits,

Culprits, like poiſonous Adders deaf, we find:

In *Biſcay*'s Bay who chides the raging Wind?

Such callous Hearts to no Impreſſion yield,

All-guarded with Corruption's ſeven-fold Shield;

Unſtung by Shame, and reſolute in Ill;

Vice is a *Python Phœbus* ne'er can kill:

Heedleſs of Satire, Sin perſiſts to reign,

As Curfews bid us leave our Fires in vain;

Poets, and Setting-Dogs, one Taſk employs,

Each *points* at Knaves or Birds, but ne'er *de-
ſtroys*;

What tho' you ſweat, complain, and rail, and
write,

The mad, luxurious Town ſins on for Spite.

Could *Boileau* to reform a Nation hope?

A *Sodom* can't be mended by a *Pope*.

To cleanse th' *Augëan* Stable tho' you toil,

Still Virtue yields to * *Heidegger* and † *Hoyle*;

Still *Britons* (Juſtice, Freedom, Conſcience ſold)

Own the ſupreme Omnipotence of Gold.

* The firſt of theſe Gentlemen was the Introducer and Manager of Maſquerades in this Kingdom, to the great and irreparable Depravation of *Englifh* Morals.

† And the latter by writing upon the Game of *Whift*, in a Mathematical and Scientifical Method, (than which nothing could be more pompoufly abſurd) extremely promoted the deſtructive Practiſe of Gaming.

Carmen

Carmen Paraphrasticum in ECCLE-SIASTICI Caput XLIII^{um}.

DÆdaleam Mundi Molem quâ condidit Arte
    Omnipotens, Rerumque inſtruxit divite cultû!
Quantus mane novâ Sol Carcere miſſus Eöo
Emicat, & læti pandit per cærula Cœli
Purpureum Jubar, & pallentes diſcutit Umbras!
Per matutino canentia Rore Vireta
Continuò Pecudum ſaltat laſciva Propago,
Et liquido Volucres latè Nemora avia mulcent
Concentû, ridetque inſueto Lumine Tellus.

At ſummâ Cœli cum Sol dominatur in Arce,
Non ultrà videas lætari Armenta per Herbas
Arentes; Sylvæ ſilucre; & languidus Æſtû
Antra petit viridi Paſtor ſtillantia Muſco.

Quin

Quin cum tantus Honos, cum tanta Potentia Soli

     est,

Vi majore viget Deus, & graviore superbit

Numine, qui Solem posuit, jussitque perennem

Ire redire Viam per Cœli immania Templa.

Ille etiam Lunam nitidâ Face jussit obire

Nocturnas vigilem Excubias, fidamque Labores

Maluit alternos certum renovare per Orbem.

Non illâ signum Cœlo formosius alto

Suspicitur, circum pandant utcunque Cohortes,

Fulgentes Stellarum Exercitus Ordine vasto,

Et Luce effusâ cœlestia conserat Arva.

Aspice quo puras subtexit Lumine Nubes,

Obliquo stringens humentia Prata Nitore

                        Vespere

Vespere sub verno, centumque Coloribus ardet

Purpureus Jovis Arcus, & amplo amplectitur Orbe

Æthereos Tractus, atque obsidet undique Cœlum!

Scilicet ipse Deus tanto Curvamine jussit

Effundi, ingentique Manû per Concava flexit.

    Quis potis est dignum pollenti Pectore Carmen

Condere pro Rerum Majestate, hisque peractis?

Quisve valet Verbis tantùm ut laudare *Jehovam*

Pro Meritis tentet?—Quis Cœlorum intima vidit

Quà Solio radiante nitet Deus? infinitum

Pingere quî posset Numen Sermonis Egestas

Humani, mortalis Citharæque infracta Loquela?

A

A

RUNIC ODE:

Taken from the

Second Volume of Sir William Temple's
MISCELLANIES.

ARGUMENT.

Regner Ladbrog, *a King of one of the Northern Nations, being mortally stung by a Viper, before the Venom had reach'd his Vitals, broke out into the following Verses.*

I.

YES—'tis decreed my Sword no more

Shall smoke and blush with hostile Gore;

To my great Father's Feasts I go,

Where luscious Wines for ever flow,

Which

Which from the hollow Sculls we drain,

Of Kings in furious Combat flain.

II.

Death, to the Brave a bleft Refort,

Brings us to awful *Odin*'s Court;

Where with old Warriors mix'd we dwell,

Recount our Wounds, our Triumphs tell;

Me, will they own as bold a Gueft,

As e'er in Battle bar'd my Breaft.

Another.

Another, on the same SUBJECT.

AT length appears the wish'd-for Night,
　　When my glad Soul shall take her Flight;

Tremble my Limbs, my Eye-balls start,

The Venom's busy at my Heart.

Hark! how the solemn * Sisters call,

And point aloft to *Odin*'s Hall!

I come, I come, prepare full Bowls,

Fit Banquet for heroic Souls:

What's Life?—I scorn this idle Breath,

I smile in the Embrace of Death!

　　　　　* Call'd by the *Goths, Dysæ.*

VERA

VERA FELICITAS.

QUA frondens Ilex annosâ amplectitur Umbrâ

    Congeſtum Culmen Ceſpite, Paſtor agit.

Non illum Populi Faſces, non Purpura tangit,

    Non Regum cæco Vulnere torquet Honos:

Mane novâ properat per Campos Rore vigentes,

    Et clauſas alacri Voce reviſit Oves·

Mox æſtum vitat ſub Ramis Arboris altæ,

    Quà viridem pandit roſcida Ripa Torum.

Pocula ſunt liquidi Fontes, Lymphæque ſalubres,

    Inque levi inſtruitur Gramine prompta Dapes.

Nunc vacuam argutâ ſolatur Arundine Mentem,

    Nunc Muſco in molli Membra Sopore levat:

Donec

Donec oves tandem conſtructa ad Ovilia ſparſas

    Cogere, tranquilli Veſperis Hora monet.

Jamque aures vaɤio permulſus Murmure, lӕto

    Corde, humilem repetit nota per Arva Larem:

Hunc Opibus ditet Fortuna benignior amplis,

    Maluerit ſolitӕ Limina fida Caſӕ.

O D E

TO

S L E E P.

I.

O Gentle, feather-footed *Sleep*,
  In drowsy Dews my Temples steep ;

Softly waving o'er my Head,

Thy Care-beguiling Rod of Lead :

O leave thy Bed of balmy Flow'rs,

And waken all thy dewy Pow'rs,

And wafted on the silent Wing,

The Dreams, thy little People bring !

II.

II.

Let ſobbing Grief, and midnight Feaſt,

Comus, and loudly-laughing *Jeſt*,

Never near my Couch appear,

Nor whiſtling Whirlwinds wound my Ear,

In Heav'n's avenging Anger ſent,

To ſhake the ſhatter'd Battlement,

From whence the melancholy Owl,

To wake the Wolf is wont to howl:

III.

But whiſpering Show'rs from off the Eaves,

Softly dripping on the Leaves,

Mix'd with the mildly-ſtirring Wind,

Shall woo to reſt my weary Mind;

M 2   Now

Now *Silence* o'er the midnight Ground,

Slowly walks his folemn Round,

In Mead or Foreft, Dale or Hill,

Commanding Nature to be ftill.

IV.

Kind *Somnus*, from the lofty Dome

To my low Cottage deign to come,

Leave murd'rous Tyrants' filken Beds,

No Poppies pour on guilty Heads,

While wailing Ghofts their Slumbers break,

That round their trembling Curtains fhriek,

While Thoughts of many a Wretch oppreft,

With Terror tear the troubled Breaft.

V.

Cramm'd with diftrefsful Bread, the Hind

With weary Limbs and vacant Mind,

By

By buzzing Night-Flies hufht, requires

No lulling Sounds from *Lydian* Lyres;

Rock'd on the high and giddy Maft,

Regardlefs of the wint'ry Blaft,

How happy the wet Sea-boy lies,

While fweeteft Slumbers feal his Eyes.

VI.

Such Joys the virtuous Bofom crown,

While Kings and Statefmen tofs on Down:

Somnus, to me fuch Joys impart,

Balm of hurt Minds, O footh my Heart:

Lapt in the Folds of foft Repofe,

We lofe our Labours, Pangs, and Woes;

Thy opiate Influence we blefs,

Parent of Forgetfulnefs!

VII.

VII.

Place me, kind God, in lively Dream

Near smooth *Iliſſus'* winding Stream.

In Olive-ſhade, with raviſht Ear,

While *Plato*'s Voice I seem to hear:

Or from the green, *Athenian* Mead

To the high *Roman* Forum lead,

Where *Tully*'s Tongue with Force divine

Confounds pale, trembling *Catiline*.

T O

Mr. *ADDISON,*

Occasioned by his Return from Hanover *with the Lord* Halifax.

Written 1700.

O For a Muse of Fire and lofty Style,
  To hail Thee welcome to thy native Soil!
Just Art is to my infant Muse unknown,
Let then the Subject for the Verse attone.

 Int'rest, that fickle Weathercock of State,
As Party prompts extorts or Praise or Hate;
True, Sterling Merit Prejudice outweighs,
Unblemisht Worth claims universal Praise;

Your

Your Favourite's juft Encomium you may boaft,

Since Factions ftrive who fhall applaud you moft.

Amaz'd we fee your finifht Lines impart,

At once the Hero's and the Poet's Art:

How nervous ev'ry Line, and yet how fweet!

Th' harmonious Whole how ev'ry where compleat!

'Tho' bold, correct and polifht is thy Song,

Sublime, yet eafy; elegant, yet ftrong:

The beauteous Graces fearcht all Nature round,

At length accomplifht *Addifon* they found;

There happy in a proper Manfion reft,

And make a Temple of his tuneful Breaft.

Methinks I fee great *Philip*'s greater Son,

And hear him wifh *Achilles*' Fate his own;

With

With Envy he admires th' immortal Man,

And Emulation boils in ev'ry Vein;

Happy (says He) who such high Praise receiv'd,

And eterniz'd in sacred *Homer* liv'd.

But happier *Marlbrô*, when fierce Winters come,

And *Anna* calls her conquering Hero home;

Finds here your Muse his matchless Acts rehearse,

While *Danube* choakt with Dead o'erflows the mighty

   Verse;

He more than sees what you so warmly write,

And gladly thinks himself again in Fight;

Again his Sword, imperial Gift, unsheaths,

And dauntless all around distributes Deaths,

With secret Pleasure vanquishes again,

A second *Blenheim* boasts, a more compleat Campaign.

Nor

Nor is great *Addison* confin'd to War,

His copious Muse makes softer Themes his Care;

By Him describ'd our Bards distinguisht shine,

In Him alone their mingled Talents join.

When *Ovid*'s moving Muse his Verse inspires,

Himself has what in *Dryden* he admires;

In all so just, so easy too in all,

That Art and Nature mutually prevail:

Your Style, Souls, Thoughts, and Numbers so

    agree,

You're his Interpreter no more, but He.

How can we *Maro*'s labouring Bees forget,

Each happy Word is as their Honey sweet!

                 Your

Your Course unwearied you our *Phœbus* run,

And Oh like Him retire, and leave us oft alone!

We mourn your Absence, when We read in You,

What All admire, what's follow'd but by Few,

And by None equal'd——but thy *Montague!*

With him *Germania*'s wondering States you see,

The blest *Achates* of his Embassy.

Hesperian Fields have once enjoy'd you too,

That much to *Virgil* owe, but more to You:

Thus *Homer* travel'd, thus where-e'er he came,

Contending Cities ow'd to Him their Fame;

As you his Art, you may their Strife revive,

And for your Birth more than seven Cities strive.

O leave no more, great Man, thy native Land,

Thy *Rhedycina*'s Tears her Son demand;

Oft

Oft I frequent the *Cherwell*'s winding Stream,

Make That my *Helicon*, and You my Theme.

How pleas'd I seek the solemn Shades alone,

And say, Here sung harmonious *Addison*:

Beneath this Oak in Summer-noons has stood,

Lay on this Bank attentive to the Flood.

As the fond Nymph soon finds by conscious Flame,

The wounded Tree that bears her Lover's Name,

So Bards by Instinct led, frequent this Scene,

Nor barely know, but feel where you have been.

Monarch of Poets! while such Bliss I boast,

My Muse is in tumultuous Rapture lost:

Transported with a Patriot-Poet's Worth,

But Language fails to give th' Ideas Birth.

From

From the *Thirteenth* ODE *of the Second* BOOK *of* HORACE.

*P*Roſerpine's Empire glimmer'd o'er my Sight,

    And dim *Elyzium* ſhed a faint Delight;

Where *Sappho*'s bleſt! who warbling plaintive Strains,

Melodious of her Country-Maids complains;

Alcæus too, who ſings of Flight and War,

Whoſe ſwelling Lyre to deeper Rage would dare;

In ſacred Silence chain'd, the Ghoſts around,

Aſtoniſht ſtare, and hang upon the Sound;

Of Kings depos'd the Throngs rejoice to hear,

And liſt'ning drink the Warblings in their Ear;

What Wonder? ſince the triple-headed Beaſt,

Starting—lops down his Ears; and lull'd to Reſt,

Erinnys' Serpents ſleep upon her Breaſt.

                         Nor

Nor now the wonted Chafe *Orion* heeds,

Nor now beneath his Hand the Lion bleeds,

The Sorrow-foothing Sounds *Prometheus* pleafe,

And *Tantalus* delude, and foften into Eafe.

VERSES

VERSES

LEFT ON

A Lady's TOILETTE.

WHY will young *Flavia*, all-accomplisht
      Fair,

Curl, powder, stick with Gems her jetty Hair?

Swell with a Hoop her painted Peacock-Tail,

Big as a vaulted Dome, or bellying Sail?

Why twinkle Diamonds on that snowy Breast,

Why are those faultless Limbs in Velvets drest?

Let *Bestia* patch and trick her out with Art,

In Crape or Cotton Beauty strikes the Heart:

What if too Gold adorn the artless Frame,

A *Titian*'s glowing Tints are still the same;

                        Rich

Rich Spice ne'er lofes its Perfumes or Sweets,

Tho' wrapt in dull *Laurafter*'s Birthday Sheets:

Arts that embellifh Life none difcommend,

If duly check'd to no Excefs they tend:

The Peer fhould differ from grofs, unbred Swain,

Gay, but not glittering; polite, but plain.

Thus *Raphael* joins Simplicity with Grace,

Beauteous, not glaring is each Limb and Face,

While artlefs Dawbers think they gain the Prize,

Who tire with Gems and Silks the dazled Eyes.

THE

THE
GLUTTON.

FAT, pamper'd *Porus*, eating for Renown,

    In Soups and Sauces melts his Manors down;

Regardless of his Heirs, with mortgag'd Lands,

Buys Hecatombs of Fish and Ortolans;

True Judge of Merit, most disdainful looks

On Chiefs and Patriots when compar'd to Cooks;

With what Delight Pigs whipt to Death he crams,

Or fatten'd Frogs, or Essences of Hams;

For fifty thousand Tongues of Peacocks sighs,

Mix'd with the Brains of Birds of Paradise;

Loud ring the Glasses, powder'd Footmen run,

He eats, drinks, surfeits, still eats, is undone!

Sees

Sees the swoln Glutton in terrific State,

Behind his Chair what dire Diseases wait?

There tottering *Gout*, and white-tongu'd *Fever* stand,

Big *Dropsy*, with full Goblets in his Hand,

Asthma thick-panting for short Gasps of Breath,

And *Apoplexy*, fiercest Friend of Death.

Sweeter the lonely Hermit's simple Food,

Who in lone Caves, or near the rushy Flood,

With eager Appetite, at early Hours,

From maple Dish salubrious Herbs devours:

Soft drowsy Dews at Eve his Temples steep,

And happy Dreams attend his easy Sleep:

Wak'd by the Thrush to neighbouring Vales he goes,

To mark how sucks the Bee, how blooms the Rose;

What latent Juice the trodden Herbage yields,

Wild Nature's Physic in the flowery Fields.

With

With Temperance footh'd each folitary Day,

Free, innocent, and eafy, fteals away,

Till Age down bends him to the friendly Grave,

No Fafhion's Dupe, no powerful Paffion's Slave.

N 2   O D E

ODE

TO

TASTE.

LEAVE not *Britannia*'s Isle; since *Pope* is
 fled

To meet his *Homer* in *Elysian* Bowers,

What Bard shall dare resume

His various-sounding Harp?

Let not resistless Dulness o'er us spread

Deep *Gothic* Night; for lo! the Fiend appears,

To blast each blooming Bay

That decks our barren Shores.

Say

Say beauteous Queen of Life-refining Arts,

Who wont to vifit oft at midnight Hour

  Sweet *Virgil*'s laurell'd Tomb

  On *Naples*' fertile Shore:

Say where thy Dwelling is? or on the Banks

Of fmooth *Iliffus*, fage-infpiring Stream,

  Where *Plato* thought of old,

  And hoar *Mufæus* walk'd!

Still doft thou tread the facred Ground where once

Thy Votaries, or ftrung the golden Lyre,

  Or taught the moral Song

  Of fweet Philofophy?

Or in fome ruin'd Temple doft thou dwell

Of ancient *Rome*, deferted of the World,

  Where proftrate lies in Duft

  The fhapely Column's Height;

     Where

Where thou may'ft ftill behold with raptur'd Eye

The beauteous Arts of fair Antiquity

    That ftill can charm the Mind,

    Tho' fmote by Time's rough Hand.

When Man a Savage wander'd in the Woods

(As hoar Tradition tells) in ancient Days,

    Wont from the laden Oak

    To fhake his barb'rous Food;

Thy Pow'r reduc'd him from his native Wilds

And to the foft Civilities of Life

    Subdu'd his ftubborn Heart;

    And taught to raife the Dome

Well-archt, to ftring the Lyre, the breathing Buft

To form, and guide the Pencil, Heav'n-born Arts

    That harmonize the Mind,

    And fit for focial Joys.

                Thee

Thee once thou faireſt Daughter of the Muſe

The *Goth* ſtern-looking bound in cruel Chains,

  And gor'd with many a Wound

  Thy bleeding Boſom fair,

When pouring o'er *Italia*'s tempting Plains

With Hand profane thy Temples he deform'd,

  And all thy beauteous Domes

  Hurl'd wildly to the Ground!

STANZAS

ON THE

PSALMS.

I.

NOT the Songs that nobly tell,

    How *Troy* was fackt, and *Rome* began,

Not the Numbers that reveal

The Wars of Heav'n to falling Man;

II.

    Can boaft that true celeftial Fire,

That equal Strength and Eafe,

    Or with fuch various Charms confpire,

To move, to teach, to pleafe.

III.

III.

Those Complaints how sadly sweet,

Which weeping Seraphim repeat;

Those Prayers how happily preferr'd,

Which God himself inspir'd and heard.

IV.

Ye partial Wits no longer boast

Of *Pindar*'s Fire in *David*'s lost!

Who to the *Hebrew* Harp must yield,

As *Jove* by great *Jehovah* is excell'd.

AVARO.

A V A R O,

A TALE.

FAST by the *Trent* (whose Gods this Fable
  tell)

A Knight in cooly Shades chose once to dwell;

Secure, in what his prosp'rous Vices gain'd,

Each Morn he vaunting view'd his Length of Land,

His Hills of silver Chalk, his Vales of golden Sand.

As on a Time, he lost his early Hounds

Far from the Musick of the choral Sounds;

Sudden he views some Shepherd's straw-built Cell,

Rich in a Barn, a Hen-roost, and a Well;

Then eye's the Swain, as to his Flock he calls,

And whistling lures 'em from their hurdl'd Walls;

Obedient

Obedient to the Tune they trot along

And careful fingle out their plaintive Young;

With fhorter Trips thefe bound upon the Plain,

Start at the Knight——but play around their Swain.

Their Swain obferv'd how free they liv'd from Want,

And wifh'd himfelf from them could learn Content:

In vain: a thoufand Cares promote his Grief,

So, (hailing firft the Knight) he afk'd Relief:

In vain; the Knight (tho' hail'd) refus'd to grant,

And thought no Swain would condefcend to want;

Then told how well the rural Life was known,

The rural Life preferring to his own;

How oft himfelf would range a-down the Hill,

And fnuff the new-built Hay-cocks ftrawb'ry Smell,

Well pleas'd to hear their Jefts the drolling Rufticks

    tell.

Nor leſs would 'tend the Weanlings, when they play,

And how himſelf was once the King of *May*;

Then when the Swain but beg'd his preſent Aid,

Left Ills unſeen his wint'ry Age invade,

Courage! (ſaid he) like Stars like Fate aſſign,

Thy Life ſhall ſtill from Want be free as mine.

  Unweeting Knight! he mourns his flying Bliſs:

All as *Polycrates* his Fate was his!

For Heav'n averſe rebuk'd ſuch boaſtful Pride,

And where he once the lowly Swain deny'd,

Himſelf (alas the while!) begs now to be ſupply'd!

So hard another's Want will win Belief!

So Pride foretels we ne'er can need Relief!

CUPID

CUPID acquitted,
A TALE.

Whenever *Jove* renews Mankind,

He makes *A Will* for ev'ry Mind.

This Gift is *different* in *Moſt*,

But *ſeldom* is by Any *loſt*.

Some Folks—(now let who can deny it)

Give all they have to gratify it:

Some, to ſubdue, divide their Wills,

Like Rivers cut in little Rills,

That leſſen to a ſhallow Maze,

And feebly run a Hundred Ways:

The Wizard thus, (in Days of Yore)

That thought to lay th' *Infernal Pow'r*,

I

In

In Pieces broke his Magic Switch,

But found A Devil rofe from Each.

Yet Some a Better Courfe purfue.——

——But to my *Tale*;—Mufe! What fay You?

Why, *That* is plain, and fhort, and new.

    Some Years ago One *Aftrophil*

Was born and fitted with A *Will*;

No Matter Who he was, or What,

A Will He had;—I'm fure of *That* :

About that Time fair *Stella* too

(GODS!—Who does not fair *Stella* know?)

Was form'd The Wonder of Her Kind,

And had *Her proper Will* affign'd.

Their Wills were ftamp't fo like (fays Fame)

That Both were only Not the Same:

I

                                             Thefe

These help'd the *Poets* in their Trade,

POPE's Similies by These were made;

Hence too his Rhimes for ever hit,

Made (by These *Wills*) exactly fit.

In short, for Virtues, or for Follies,

These Wills were *Pairs*, or *Twins*, or *Tallies*.

Well! *Hymen*— (as you guess, no doubt,

And you guess right) —soon found 'em out,

   And bound 'em fast, like two chain'd Books,

And, ever and anon was peeping,

   To see if Time impair'd their Looks,

Or, if They alter'd, in *His* keeping.

They alter'd Not. But *Love*, one Day,

Convey'd (it seems) *One Will* away;

And *Which* was *That?*—Nay!—Who can say?

For *Love* Himſelf, with All his Art,

Could *not* tell Whoſe was Whoſe a-part.

Now *Hymen*, you muſt think, complain'd,

That, " Tho' *Himſelf Both Wills* had chain'd,

" Yet One—Ah! *Only One* remain'd!—

" That *Stella* now, or *Aſtro-phil*,

" Might come upon him for their *Will*:

" That, therefore *Jove* the Cauſe ſhould hear,

" And pray'd," That *Cupid* might appear.

HE Did: And roundly took his Oath

That *Jove* made—*but One Will* for *Both*.

His ſtrange Surprize He then declar'd,

" 'Twas Hard, He needs muſt ſay, 'twas hard,

" That HE ſhould be involv'd in Strife,

" HE ſeldom troubl'd *Man* and *Wife*.

" And

" And—What *in this* Cafe He might do—

" *They* ne'er would blame him for't he knew;

" And—Why then, *Hymen?* Why fhould You?

" Still; you fhall never have your Ends,

" For *This Dear Couple* were my *Friends!*"

With That—He turns to *Swain* and *Spoufe*,

And fmiles, and leers, and fooths, and vows,

" For *His* Part He would ferve 'em ftill,"

Then afks 'em (with A *Courtier*'s Skill)

" If ever *Either mifs'd their Will?*"

So, 'Tis *Their* Bufinefs Now to fpeak,

And pray—What Anfwer fhall They make?

THREE

THREE
EPIGRAMS
Tranflated from the Greek.

ADVERTISEMENT.

THE following Pieces are a Pattern of the Simplicity fo much admir'd in the *Grecian* Writings, fo foreign to the prefent prevailing Tafte, to the Love of Modern Witticifm, and *Italian* Conceit.

On a CAVE.

From the Greek *of* Anyta, *a* Lefbian *Poetefs.*

COME, Traveller, this hollow Rock beneath,

    While in the Leaves refrefhing Breezes breath ;

Retire, to calm the Rage of burning Thirft,

In thefe cool Streams that from the Cavern burft.

An

[195]

An *Offering* to PAN.

From Theocritus.

*D*APHNIS the Fair, that with the *Doric*
Strains

Of his sweet Pipe could charm the listening Swains,

These Emblems of his Office and his Art,

To PAN presents, a Crook and barbed Dart,

A Stag's rough Hide, and with this Pastoral Pipe,

That bore his rustic Food, a Leathern Scrip.

To

To DAPHNIS *ſleeping.*

From Theocritus.

WHILE you, my DAPHNIS, on the leafy
Bed,

To Slumber ſweet recline your weary Head,

While on each Hill is plac'd the frequent Net,

Thee wanton PAN purſues with eager Feet;

With him SYLVANUS, crown'd with Ivy pale,

Thy cooling Cavern ſeeks o'er Hill and Dale.

O fly; prevent their rude reſiſtleſs Hands,

And burſt ambroſial Slumber's magic Bands.

A

A

PASTORAL

On the Death of BION.

From the Greek of MOSCHUS.

YE Vales, and *Doric* Floods, or Fount, or Rill,

　　Lament with me the much lov'd *Bion* dead;

Ye Forests pour your Plaints, ye Flourets mourn;

Utter, ye Hyacinths, the baleful Words

That on your velvet Bells infcrib'd are feen;

Be clad, ye Rofes, in fad Purple's Robe;

Dead is the Pride of Swains, and rural Song.

Begin, *Sicilian* Mufe, the plaintive Lay.

　Ye Poplar-fhrouded Nightingales that oft

In midnight Hour complain, the dreary Tale

　　　　　　　To

To liſtening *Arethuſa*'s Waves prolong,

And that with him each *Doric* Muſe is fled.

Begin, *&c.*

Ye Swans that warble ſweet on *Strymon*'s Bank

Come, ſteep in bitter Tears your ſorrowing Song,

And tell in Notes like his th' *Æagrian* Maids,

And *Bacchus*' Nymphs that haunt *Biſtonian* Hills,

That *Doria*'s Vales their *Orpheus* dear have loſt!

Begin, *&c.*

No more the lovely Shepherd ſooths his Herd

With ſoft-voic'd Flute, beneath ſome ample Oak

At Eaſe reclin'd: But in black *Pluto*'s Bow'r

Pours forth to griſly Ghoſts *Lethëan* Lays,

While here above each Mountain ſilent ſtands,

And

3

And his deferted Herds in Mutt'rings hoarfe,

And fullen Lowings moan, nor deign to feed.

   Begin, &c.

   Thy cruel Fate, dear Swain, *Apollo* wept,

Thee too *Priapus* Sable-mantled mourn'd;

And *Pan* furrounded with his Satyr-train

Sigh'd fore, nor joy'd to lead the merry Dance;

Wept the mild *Naiads* in their coral Caves;

Nor Echo more from her far-winding Grot

Is heard to fing, fince now no more thy Verfe,

And wonted tuneful Notes fhe can prolong.

   Begin, &c.

   At thy fad Death the fympathizing Trees,

Dropt their half-ripen'd Fruits, and fading Flowers,

      Hung

Hung down their blasted Blooms; the pining

    Flocks

Refus'd the milky Stream, nor more the Bee

With Thyme enrich'd his Nectar-streaming Cell.

    Begin, *&c.*

    The Dolphin ne'er upon the sunny Shore

Made such deep Plaints, or in the rocky Wilds

Did *Philomel* e'er tune so sad a Dirge,

Nor Mountain-loving Swallow such sad Notes

Was heard to pour, or with such heart-felt Woe

Cëyx deplor'd her dead *Halcyóne*,

Nor *Cerylas* in the *Cærulean* Deep

Sorrow'd so deep, or in th' *Eöan* Vale

The Bird of *Memnon*, fair *Aurora*'s Son,

As

As when they wept their beſt-lov'd *Bion*'s Fate.

   Begin, &c.

   Ye Nightingales, and Swallows ſwift, that oft

Have heard delighted his heart-thrilling Lays,

Whom ſeated in your leafy Groves he wont

To teach ſweet Notes, reſponſive now repeat

The Voice of Woe, re-echoing thro' the Vale,

Join too ye Doves your ſadly-pleaſing Lays.

   Begin, &c.

   Who now, for ever dear, will tune thy Pipe?

Who to their Lip apply thy ſacred Reed

Advent'rous? But to *Pan* the precious Gift

I'll bear, nor haply will he dare inſpire

Thy Reed, leſt thee ſuperior he ſhould prove.

   Begin, &c.   Thy

Thy Loſs the green-hair'd *Galathëa* mourns,

Who lov'd with thee upon the ſea-beat Shore,

To ſit enraptur'd with thy magic Verſe.

For ſweeter ſat than *Polypheme*'s thy Lay

Flow'd thro' her Ear; ſhe fled the Cyclop-ſwain;

But ever to thy Song ſhe haſten'd ſwift,

With dimply Cheek, and Looks of fond Deſire.

No more ſhe now regards old *Nereus*' Bow'r,

But on the bare Sand ſits, and tends thy Flock.

    Begin, *&c.*

With thee the Muſe's choiceſt Joys are fled,

No more the Virgin's luſcious Kiſs delights;

Quench'd is the Lamp of Love, and at thy Tomb

The weeping *Cupids* ſprinkle freſheſt Flow'rs;

To *Venus* wert thou ſweeter, gentleſt Swain,

Than

Than the laſt Kiſs which on the clay-cold Lip

Of her *Adonis* dead the Goddeſs preſt.

Come, *Meles*, hither turn thy ſedge-crown'd Head,

Renew thy wonted Voice of baleful Woe;

That erſt around thy ſadden'd Banks was heard,

And echoing fill'd blue *Neptune*'s diſtant Shores;

When cruel Fate thy firſt-born *Homer* ſnatch'd,

Whoſe Mouth *Calliope* with Nectar dew'd.

But now thy ſecond Son demands thy Grief;

Each lov'd two fav'rite Founts.   To *Homer* dear

Was *Pindus*' ſpringing Well, while *Bion* drank

The Waves of *Arethuſe*.   This ſung the Charms

Of beauteous *Helen*, ſtrife-exciting Fair,

And the dire Wrath of *Thetis*' ſea-born Son;

While This neglected War's reſounding Trump;

Well cou'd he ſing the woodland Wanderer *Pan*;

Skill'd

Skill'd was his Hand to form the ruſtic Flute;

Nor ſeldom would he milk the ſhaggy Goat,

Or Heifer breathing Sweets.   Meantime he ſung

How ſoft the Kiſs of tender-blooming Boys;

While in his Boſom *Cupid* wont to ſleep,

And *Venus* joy'd to hear his Lays divine.

  Begin, *&c.*

Each towred City, *Bion,* thee deplores,

More heart-felt Plaints o'er *Aſcra*'s Hills reſound

Than when Her *Heſiod* died.   *Bæotia*'s Shades

Forget their *Pindar,* and the *Lesbian* Streets

Alcæus dead, and all thy Death lament

In ſympathizing Grief; while *Paros* deigns

With louder Woe to greet thy cypreſs'd Hearſe,

Than when *Archilochus*' ſweet Tongue was ſtopt

3   By

By cruel Fate; and *Mytilene* forgets

Her beauteous *Sappho*'s wonted Lays for thine.

* * * * * * * * *   *Quædam defunt.*

In *Teios*' foft *Anacreon* bears the Palm,

Theocritus in *Syracufe* is fam'd,

My mournful Mufe delights *Aufonian* Swains,

Nor to the *Sylvan* Lay difdains to ftoop;

Which eager from thy tuneful Mouth fhe caught,

Oft raptur'd with the Sound.   The fhining Stores

Let others, narrow-foul'd poffefs, while I

Thy Lays inherit, and thy *Doric* Art.

   Begin, *&c.*

Tho' nipt by Winter's Blaft the Mallow fades,

And twining Parfley, Pride of Gardens, feels

Th' untimely Froft; yet each with Verdure frefh

Renew

Renew their Bloom, and with the Spring return.

But Man, tho' Strength and Wisdom stamp him
      Great,

When once the beaming Lamp of Life is spent,

To Caves of Darkness, subterranean Glooms,

Immers'd, in Sleep's eternal Shackles lies

Fast bound, no more to tread the Walks of Men.

Thou too to Realms of silent Night art gone,

While here above mean Bards usurp thy Reign,

Whose Brows the Muse's Laurel never bound.

    Begin, &c.

* O ruthless Hand that to thy Lips apply'd

The poisonous Cup, and baleful Draught of Death!

How cou'd the baleful Drugs approach thy Lips,

      * He was poison'd.

                       Nor

Nor ftill preferve its native noxious Gall

Unblended with the Nectar of thy Mouth?

How could the Felon drear that mix'd the Bowl

Efcape the Magic of thy tuneful Strains?

    Begin, &c.

    On each the Fates adjuft the Share of Pain,

And each receives his portion'd Lot of Grief.

O that like *Orpheus* I cou'd tread the Shades,

Or great *Ulyffes*, or brave *Hercules*,

Then wou'd thefe Eyes behold th' infernal Pow'rs

Melt at thy Song, and *Pluto*, grifly King,

To Softnefs footh'd, and murm'ring hoarfe Applaufe.

But chief to *Hecate* thy fweet Song addrefs,

And let her hear thy wonted *Doric* Songs,

For fhe of Yore the Vales of *Ætna* lov'd.

Haply

Haply deceiv'd by the mellifluous Sound,

She may return thee to thy defert Seats:

I too, my Friend, if this rude Lip was fkill'd

In Mufic's Charms, or knew to fing like thee,

Would to the Ways of darkfome *Dis* defcend,

And from dun Night redeem thy facred Shade.

A

A

PARAPHRASE

On the XIIIth *Chap. of* ISAIAH.

HIGH on the loftiest Mountain-tops, unfurl
  The Standard of Omnipotence, emblaz'd
With Pictures of Destruction: Loudly call
To Arms the starting Nations: Rouze, O Earth,
To fight my Battles, to destroy the Pride,
To crush the Head of barbarous *Babylon*.
Ye chosen Armies come! ye Instruments
Of Vengeance from remotest Regions hast!
Hark! how the Mountains eccho with the Sounds
Of trampling Hosts, of loudly-neighing Steeds,
Of bounding Chariot-wheels, that pour amain

    P   Down

Down the steep Valley, like the deaf'ning Roar

Of rushing Torrents, or the threat'ning Voice

Of mighty Thund'rings, heard from Heav'n remote.

Howl, thou devoted City, for the Lord

Sends his destroying Angels forth——a God

Becomes thy Foe, thy deep Distress shall be

Unequal'd and supreme! thy Warriors' Hearts

Shall melt within their Breasts, their feeble Hands

Shall quivering drop the useless Spear and Shield.

Astonishment, and Anguish, Sorrow, Fear,

Shall chain their Faculties and Souls, as Pains

Soul-piercing Pains the pregnant Mother seize.

The dread *Jehovah* comes——before him march

Anger and *Vengeance*: The polluted Land

Shall desolated mourn, and far away

His red Right Hand shall shrieking Sinners sweep.

Then

Then fhall the Stars of Heav'n, the glittering Gems

Of awful Night's dark Robe, the pale-ey'd Moon,

The weary Pilgrim's Friend, and the great Sun,

Who from the cryftal Portals of the Eaft

Walks forth with tenfold Brightnefs cloth'd, and
     pours

Intolerable Day, all darken'd droop.

Earth from her Orbit fhall aftonifht leap,

Heav'n rock and tremble to the Throne of God.

As the chas'd Doe to pathlefs Thickets runs,

Trembling at every Breeze, and thinks fhe hears

The fhouting Hunter, fo fhall *Babel* fly,

As a ftray Lamb on defert Mountains loft.

Th' avenging *Medes* unmov'd fhall hear the Cries

Of ravifht Wives and Virgins, from the Breafts

Of fhrieking Mothers fnatch the fucking Babe,

Smiling

Smiling in its Deftroyer's Face, and dafh

Againft the pointed Flints its mangled Bones.

The Queen of Kingdoms, the *Chaldeans* Pride,

The Glory of the Earth, great *Babel* falls,

Like burning *Sodom* in Deftruction wrapt.

From Age to Age fhall Defolation reign,

And Solitude thro' thy deferted Streets.

Then fhall no wand'ring *Arab* pitch his Tent

Frefh Pafture fearching, nor the Shepherd drive

His Flock at Eve beneath thy Ruins hoar

To fhelter; in thy widow'd Palaces

Magnific mould'ring Domes, the Defert's Sons

Wild Beafts fhall lodge; the fpotted Panther breed

In thy King's Chambers, here the Oftrich cry,

And the young Leopard fport, with Song and Dance

And Harp, where eccho'd once thy feaftful Halls.

THE

THE

REGAL DREAM.

1715.

***

The ARGUMENT.

That which gave Occasion to the Regal Dream *is a
famous Tradition mention'd in the History of*
Henry VII. *by which we are told, that He sent to
enquire after his Successors from a celebrated Pro-
phet or Necromancer, who for his Answer return'd
him this remarkable* Latin *Verse:*

Mars, Puer, Alecto, Virgo, Vulpes, Leo, Nullus.

*These Emblems the Author of the following Vision
thought fit to alter in some measure, and to add
another Line; the Whole standing thus:*

Fur, Puer, Alecto, Virgo, Vulpes, Pelicanus,

Et Caper, & Cervus, brevis & Flos, dia Columba.

P 3

'Twas

'TWAS on the Day that *Bofworth* Field was
won,

And *Glo'fter* fell, and *Richmond* wore the Crown,

When as I fat revolving in my Mind,

The Chiefs defcended from two Houfes join'd,

A balmy Slumber with a fweet Surprize,

Stole foft and filent o'er my yielding Eyes;

Fancy, officious every Part to act,

Or Nature's Landfcapes, or hiftoric Fact,

A Bower had built profufely gay and bright,

With all the Beauty that can take the Sight,

Not more enchanting that *Elyfian* Place

Where good *Æneas* faw the *Julian* Race,

An Area foon with myftic Signs was fpread,

Diverfified with Rofes White and Red:

Thither

Thither a *Sybil* call'd me from the Throng

To mark the various Figures move along:

My awe-ftruck Memory never fhall forget

Their Forms, their Names, their Numbers, and their

State.

A Robber firft, with holy Plunder fraught,

Whofe leff'ning Bags were Gold, were Duft, were

Nought.

A Youth came next, who charm'd with ev'ry Grace,

As Angels good, and O as fwift his Pace.

A Fury then, with more diforder'd Hafte,

Paft by, and dealt Deftruction as fhe paft.

Her ruffled Garments dropt with Martyr's Gore,

And in her Hand a flaming Torch fhe bore.

Not

Not so the heavenly Maid who next arose,

Admir'd by all, tho' terrible to Foes;

Whose Aim was nobler, and whose Speed was less,

Who rose to triumph, and who stay'd to bless;

A Phœnix she, that peerless liv'd and dy'd,

Nor left a Race that her great Loss supply'd.

Yet came there to fulfil her last Command,

The wisest Animal of Nature's Hand,

A tame, a peaceful, tho' a wily Fox,

Who never slew, but only fleec'd the Flocks.

Soon as he earth'd a Pelican arose,

By Friends deserted, and pursu'd by Foes;

In Both his brave Contempt of Life was shewn,

Who for the Good of Others gave his Own.

Here

Here all methought was Dark! at length appear
A Goat lafcivious, and a hunted Deer.

The *Sybil* paus'd—and her fage Art to prove,
Declar'd that Thefe would different Paffions move,
Our ufelefs Pity One, and One our lafting Love.

Now rofe a fweet Carnation's filken Flow'r,
Fruitlefs, yet fair, the Beauty of an Hour,
For poifonous *Eurus* came——its bloomy Pride,
That unexpected rofe, as quickly dy'd.

Next feem'd to dart from Heaven, a fpotlefs Dove,
Who dropt an Olive-Branch, the Type of Love;
Then all too fudden flew amid the Spheres,
And fhone a Star upon the World in Tears.

The

The Visionary Crowd that gaz'd below

All wept in Dream, and gave a Loose to Woe;

Britannia's self abandon'd to Despair,

Her azure Mantle tore, and sea-green Hair:

Deep Sorrow wak'd me from th' unfinisht Scene,

Eternally to mourn a matchless Queen.

A

FAREWELL *to* POETRY.

Nunc itaque & Versus & cætera Ludicra pono,
Quod Verum atque Decens curo & rogo & omnis in
hóc sum.　　　　　　　　　　　HOR.

*A*Rcadian Scenes adieu! in *Cyrrha*'s Vale

　　No more I wander, where with loose-rob'd

　　Nymphs

Pan and *Sylvanus* play'd, while on their Heads

The laughing *Hours* rain'd Roses; while to guide

Their nimble Feet great *Phœbus* came and touch'd,

His soul-bewitching Lyre: No more I sit

On murmuring *Aganippe*'s mossy Brink

And wait inspiring Dreams; nor Garlands weave

Of sweet *Parnassian* Flowers for *Clio*'s Head;

Nor feek the folemn Grott where *Homer* firft

Conceiv'd his mighty Scheme; from whence to catch

One Beam fwift-darted from his boundlefs Mind.

My ferious Soul thefe Woods and Walks difdains

Where my Youth rov'd: A loftier Tafk demands

My fober Hours, (that on fwift Pinions haft

To meet Eternity) to purge my Breaft

From Error's Poifons; equally to poife

The jarring Paffions; to fubdue the Thirft

Of Fame and fond Ambition; to deftroy

The bitter Seeds of Envy :——Not to fmooth

The tuneful Cadence of a polifht Line,

But harmonize my Soul; whence I may hear,

With Raptures hear, the Moral Melody,

A peaceful Confcience yields, beyond the Strains

Of *Attic* Harp, fweet as the Midnight Song

Of

Of warbling Seraphs, winged Warriors bright,

To happy, watchful Shepherds, on the Birth

Of great Meſſiah!——Theſe be now my Cares,

To leave the Muſe for Virtue; to improve

The Heart, not deck the Head with fading Crown

Of uſeleſs Bays; but chief my Soul to ſteel

With adamantine Honour, to withſtand

Corruption's Tides, while courtly Millions run

To the black Pagod of all-worſhip'd *Vice*

To offer Freedom, Conſcience, Body, Soul:

To be tho' ſingle, conſtant; and to feel

The Bliſs of Independence;—theſe are Toils

Worthy a Man and *Briton.*——Who can ſearch

For tinkling Rhymes, when frowning *Virtue* points

To ſwift-wing'd Time?—At Cloſe of Evening cool

What haſty Pilgrim, who long, pathleſs Wilds

2

Muſt

Muſt traverſe e'er black Night deſcend, would ſtop

And ſit beneath the branching Beech to hear

The ſweet Songs of thick-warbling *Philomel*,

Tho' ev'ry moving Trill be ſteep'd in Tears.

ODE

O D E

ON THE

DEATH *of the* AUTHOR.

By a LADY.

I.

ACCEPT, O sacred Shade, this artless Verse,

And kindly, O ye mourning Friends, for-

bear,

To dear disdaining from his decent Herse,

All I can give except the tender Tear:

He must not lie in his cold Grave, among

Poor shrieking Ghosts, unprais'd, unwept, unsung.

II.

II.

Ah! where was I when fiercely-frowning Death,

    With brandiſht Dart ſtood at ſtill Midnight nigh,

Why came I not to catch thy dying Breath,

    And cloſe with trembling Hand thy languid Eye?

And on my ſad Breaſt lay thy drooping Head,

And bath with Tears thy Hand ſo cold and dead?

III.

Thee do I view in yonder flying Cloud,

    Or do I hear thee in the hollow Wind,

Or doſt thou ſtill ſleep in thy ſable Shroud,

    Where the dread Judgment-Trumpet Thee ſhall

      find:

O till that Day, ye pitying Angels come,

Shield with your Wings, and ſing around his Tomb.

                         IV.

IV.

But if advanc'd to Heav'n's empyreal Height,

    Above with glorious martyr'd Saints to live,

'Midſt heav'nly Hymns, and Harps, and Viſions

    bright,

    And all the Joys a ſmiling God can give ;

O be my watchful Guardian Angel ſtill,

Save me from ſlaviſh Vice, from Folly, and from Ill.

J. W.

O D E

ON THE

DEATH *of the* AUTHOR.

NO more of Mirth and rural Joys,

    The gay Description quickly cloys,

In melting Numbers, sadly flow,

I tune my alter'd Strings to Woe;

Attend, *Melpomene*, and with thee bring

Thy tragic Lute, *Euphranor*'s Death to sing.

Fond wilt thou be his Name to praise,

For oft' thou heard'st his skilful Lays;

Isis for him soft Tears has shed,

She plac'd her Ivy on his Head;

                                       Chose

I

Chose him, strict Judge, to rule with steady Reins,

The vigorous Fancies of her listening Swains.

With Genius, Wit, and Science blest,

Unshaken Honour arm'd his Breast,

Bade him, with virtuous Courage wise,

Malignant *Fortune*'s Darts despise;

Him, ev'n black *Envy*'s venom'd Tongues commend,

As Scholar, Pastor, Husband, Father, Friend.

For ever sacred, ever dear,

O much-lov'd Shade accept this Tear;

Each Night indulging pious Woe,

Fresh Roses on thy Tomb I strew,

And wish for tender *Spenser*'s moving Verse,

Warbled in broken Sobs o'er *Sydney*'s Herse;

Let

Let me to that deep Cave refort,

Where *Sorrow* keeps her filent Court,

For ever wringing her pale Hands,

While dumb *Misfortune* near her ftands,

With downcaft Eyes the *Cares* around her wait,

And *Pity* fobbing fits before the Gate.

Thus ftretch'd upon his Grave I fung,

When ftrait my Ears with Murmur rung,

A diftant, deaf, and hollow Sound

Was heard in folemn Whifpers round ——

" Enough, dear Youth!——tho' wrapt in Blifs above,

" Well-pleas'd I liften to thy Lays of Love."

Jos. WARTON.

F I N I S.

Errors of the Prefs.

PAGE 15. Line 7. *for* ftedfaft Thought, *read* folemn Thought. P. 41. l. 1. *f.* twifting, *r.* burfting. P. 54. l. 8. *f.* & Vatem, *r.* ad Vatem. Ibid. l. 11. *f.* novus, *r.* novas. P. 55. l. 8. *f.* fructæ, *r.* fractæ. P. 56. l. 4. *f.* Libertus, *r* Libertas. P. 81. l. 1. *f.* then, *r.* there.